Christb in the ~~~ ~~~

Promised, Patterned, and Present

Douglas Van Dorn

Christ in the Old Testament

Promised, Patterned, and Present

Douglas Van Dorn

Waters of Creation Publishing
Dacono, Colorado

Originally published as *From the Shadows to the Savior: Christ in the Old Testament* © 2015. This is a revised and expanded edition.

Unless otherwise noted, references are from the *English Standard Version* (ESV) of the Bible.

Cover Design: Doug, Breanna, and Alesha Van Dorn

ISBN: 978-0-9862376-6-9 (Waters of Creation Publishing)

Contents

Contents

Other Books by Waters of Creation

Christ in All Scripture Series

For more information, articles, radio shows, and broadcasts go to: dougvandorn.com

Dedicated to:

Uncle Norman and all my other uncles and aunts—
each of whom, in his overwhelming kindness,
God has graciously seen fit to savingly reveal him Son.

Forewords

CHRIST IN THE OLD TESTAMENT? It doesn't take a seminary degree to know that Jesus wasn't born until just prior to the first century. In fact, the Bible doesn't even deal with Jesus' birth until the book of Matthew in the New Testament! Or, perhaps we've been reading it wrong this whole time...

Pastor Van Dorn has provided a marvelous introduction to a study of Christ in the Old Testament. The eternal Logos always has been and forever will be the second member of the Trinity, so shouldn't we expect to see him at work throughout all of redemptive history? Even Jesus himself made clear to some very confused disciples that he was the one they had been reading about all along (Luke 24:27, 44-47). Jesus said in John 5:39, "You [Jewish people] diligently study the Scriptures [which at that time were the 39 books of the Old Testament]...These are the Scriptures that testify about me."

Most Christians today assume the Old Testament patriarchs heard booming voices from heaven and had numerous dreams and visions directed by God for their instruction and wisdom. And while these instances

surely occurred, when we look a little closer we see
more to the story. Have you ever considered that just
maybe God was with the people, face-to-face?

The Old Testament Scriptures are just as much
about Jesus as the New. Pastor Van Dorn provides
convincing, biblical evidence that unveils the identity
of the Angel of the Lord, the one who the ancient Jews
called the second voice in heaven, and who the Bible
(more often than you might realize) refers to as the
Logos of God. As you take the journey to discover
Christ in the Old Testament, you will delight in the
seamless continuity and progressive revelation of the
entirety of Scripture. May your affections for Jesus be
stirred up all the more as you discover the second person on every page of Scripture!

NICK KENNICOTT
PH.D. CANDIDATE, Faulkner University
PASTOR, REDEEMER BAPTIST CHURCH, RINCON, GA

*** *** ***

TO AND FOR A CHRISTIAN, there can be nothing more
important than Christ Himself. At least that's the way
it *ought* to be. How many of us at some point or another
have either heard the song, "You Are My All In All",
or sang it ourselves? Yet, is it true? Is Jesus *really* our All
in All – even in the Old Testament? One would think,
that for a Christian, seeing Jesus in the book that He
authored would be easy enough. Sadly, for many, not

only is it difficult, but it's sometimes even sneered at. The very thought is even addressed as if it's some sort of insult to mention Jesus in the context of the Old Testament unless something very specific about Him is mentioned in the New Testament regarding it. Instead of rejoicing to find the Savior throughout all of Scripture – especially the Old Testament -, oftentimes we act like the Sheriff of Nottingham chasing Robin Hood through Sherwood Forest. We "think" the bandit might be among the trees somewhere, but at most He appears as a ghost or legend.

When did we move away from the hermeneutic that Jesus Himself used (Himself being the key hermeneutic)? Without Jesus, there IS no Old Testament. This is what makes the book you are about to read so important. Can you imagine seeing Hamlet, without Hamlet? Or how interesting would "The Phantom of the Opera" be without the phantom? Why then would we take the main character in God's Story, and remove Him? In God's book, we find God, and not just a general reference to some general higher power, but the Triune personal God – The Father, The Son, & The Holy Spirit. But what does it say when we view over half of scripture as missing the second Person of the Trinity? This is what Doug's book does so well. In all and every aspect, he shows us the Lord of the Book in all His glory.

Worship, power, The Angel of the Lord, The Right Arm of God, The Son of God, The Very Word of God, The Law of God – all of this and more is both eloquently, and concretely discussed regarding Jesus Christ. In our present time, when so many are turning the Old Testament into Aesop's Fables, or disregarding it all together, a more important volume couldn't have been written. If the point of the Old Testament was to lead to Jesus, why wouldn't we find Him In the Old Testament? Doug answers this wholeheartedly by showing us how hard it is to NOT see Him there.

Some books aren't worth reading. Some are worth reading once. Others are worth reading time and again, and this is one of those books. Immerse yourself among the giant trees here, and see how each one shows us the Savior, making up the grand forest view of God's redemptive history. I am grateful for such a heart as Doug's in wanting to portray Jesus as all of Scripture does. Hear the Savior's voice, see the Christ's types, and read the words about Him – He who is the author of our faith. A faith that was given to us, not to conceal the Savior, but to reveal the Savior to us more and more, as we read the *entire* Bible.

SEAN KIELIAN ~ PASTOR/ELDER
SOUTHSIDE BIBLE CHURCH, CENTENNIAL, CO

Preface

Reason for This Series

I am convinced, after studying the topic of Christ in the Old Testament in some depth for the last several years, and having lived in modern conservative Reformed and Evangelical Christian circles for nearly 50 years, that too many Christians (past and present) far too often presuppose and/or superimpose a kind of Unitarian grid upon the OT. This is a very Liberal way of reading the Scripture, out of line with orthodox Christian teaching throughout history.

It isn't that this is done malevolently, for these same Christians often do see Christ in the OT in one way or another. I am not talking about a Christianity that outright denies the deity of Jesus. In fact, I'm talking about a Christianity that loves him as the *Theanthropos*—The God-man. It isn't that this is done deliberately either. At least, not usually. I would say it is more of a subconscious decision. We speak about Christ being there in type and shadow, but to say that he was actually there—*in person?* This is a hard pill for many to swallow. I had more than one professor in my conservative Baptist schooling tell the students that to see Christ or a Trinity actually there, as if any of the human authors could have deliberately written about these things when they wrote the OT books, was reading the NT back into the Old. It was eisegesis, not exegesis.

In this way, too many of us presuppose that the Jewish church did not, indeed *could not* have known the Christ to write about him actually being present in their midst. He simply wasn't there among them. At best, only the Father was. Yet, somehow, we think, they could foresee his coming. But this is a strange oxymoron, because that would seem to itself presuppose that they knew he already existed, if the Messiah they prophesied about was truly God. But if they knew he already existed, why couldn't he have known them or made himself known to them? Nevertheless, at the end of the day when we ask questions like *Job knew his Redeemer* (Job 19:25) *to be Christ?* Or *Solomon comprehended the Son of a Father who has ascended to heaven* (Prov 30:4) *was Christ?* Or *Abraham believed God* (Gen 15:6), *whom he knew to be Christ?* Not possible is a very common answer to hear.

As a case in point, there is an ancient manuscript variant in Jude 5 where one family of texts say "Jesus" lead Israel in the Exodus, while another family reads the "Lord" did it. Apparently, this discussion has been around for a long, long time. Some scribe was asking the same question: *Jude could call the Savior of the Exodus "Jesus?"* Not possible. So he changed "Jesus" to "Lord." The renowned NT scholar Bruce Metzger ran into the same skepticism I have run into in conservative circles on this very same variant when he was working on his *Textual Commentary on the Greek New Testament* in a committee with a bunch of other scholars. He wrote, "A majority of the Committee was of the opinion that the [Jesus] reading was difficult to the point of impossibility."[1]

Why? Because we presuppose it, that's why. Therefore, any OT text you can think of where a Christian has argued that we see the Trinity or Christ ("Holy, Holy, Holy" or "Let us make man in our image") must be dismissed out of hand.

This Work and Its Place in this Series

The work before you is a volume in the series: Christ in All Scripture, by Waters of Creation Publishing. At present, this series consists or will consist of the following volumes:

- *A Dissertation Concerning the Angel Who is called the Redeemer and Other Select Passages* by Peter Allix

---

[1] Bruce Manning Metzger, United Bible Societies, *A Textual Commentary on the Greek New Testament, Second Edition a Companion Volume to the United Bible Societies' Greek New Testament (4th Rev. Ed.)* (London; New York: United Bible Societies, 1994), 657.

- *Appearances of the Son of God Under the Old Testament* by John Owen
- *The Worship of the Lord Jesus Christ in the Old Testament* by Gerard De Gols
- *The Angel of the LORD in Early Jewish, Christian, and Reformation History*, a compilation of Allix, Owen, and De Gols
- *Christ in the Old Testament: Promised, Patterned, and Present* by Douglas Van Dorn
- *Jesus: Who, What, Where, When, Why?* by Douglas Van Dorn

The book before you now is the fifth book in this series. It began as a series of blogs done for the Decablog. After reading that series, several people approached me with putting it into a single offline format that could be given away or recommend to others. Originally published as *From the Shadows to the Savior: Christ in the Old Testament* (2015), it was my attempt at a very basic introduction into the potentially volume filling, and certainly life-transforming subject of Christ in the Old Testament (OT).

Since that time, I have developed that longer volume with my friend and fellow pastor Matt Foreman. We will be publishing the fuller book in the near future. This volume stands as a digestible supplement and study guide to that larger volume.

It is divided into six parts with several new sections in this updated edition. After an introduction to the topic, we talk about some New Testament (NT) passages that talk explicitly about Christ or Jesus in the OT *as a person*. The next three parts focus on Christ in the OT through various concepts such as *prophecy*, *typology*, and the *law*. The next seven parts look at different words that show us the person of Christ as he is found in the OT. Christians understood many of them to talk about Christ specifically, while even early Jews understood them to be mysteriously talking about a kind of plurality within a Godhead, a fact little known to Jews or Christians in our day. The final part is a conclusion that uses Hebrews to pull these various threads together.

It is my sincere hope and prayer that this book will find a wide readership, because the contents that lay herein are of the utmost importance and value in the continuing discussion of Christ in the Old Testament, a topic so important that Jesus says through it we have life.

DOUG VAN DORN ~ REFORMED BAPTIST CHURCH
OF NORTHERN COLORADO
(WINTER, 2019)

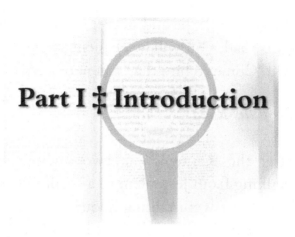

Part I ‡ Introduction

The Key and a Prayer

I WANT TO LOOK AT WHAT I believe is the key to reading the Scriptures properly. It is the key because no matter what other grid Christians may use to make the Scriptures cohere (covenant, kingdom, divine council, dispensations, etc.), this one was taught explicitly by the Lord Jesus himself as the one that leads us directly to eternal life. This makes our subject very important.

That key is to see the Second Person of the Trinity throughout the Old Testament. "You search the Scriptures because you think that in them you have eternal life," Jesus told the Pharisees. But, "It is they that bear witness about me" (John 5:39). Yet, it is not enough to read the Scripture with him at the center. We must *come to him* because of it. He continues, "Yet you refuse to come to me that you may have life"

(John 5:40). My hope and prayer is that as we travel down this road, you will be challenged anew to do as Jesus said. Come to him that you may have life.

The Emmaus Road

After the Resurrection, two disciples of Jesus were walking from Jerusalem to a small village called Emmaus. They were talking about reports of an incredible event that they did not believe. Some were saying that Jesus had actually risen from the grave. Suddenly, the Lord Jesus himself stood behind them. Prevented from recognizing who he was, he began to scold them for being so slow to believe. The basis? "'Was it not necessary that the Christ should suffer these things and enter into his glory?' And beginning with Moses and all the Prophets, he interpreted to them in all the Scriptures the things concerning himself" (Luke 24:26-27).

The word "interpreted" here is *diermeneuo*. We derive the English word "hermeneutics" from this. Hermeneutics is the art and science of biblical interpretation. A few years ago, I was talking with a friend and I asked him, "Where do you get your hermeneutic?" He was bewildered. He hadn't thought of that question before. He essentially got it from the seminary he was attending. But beyond that, he didn't have an answer. Yet, here is an explicitly taught hermeneutic from the Lord himself.

This hermeneutic is to see him in and throughout the OT. This is such an important idea for Luke that he repeats it. "'These are my words that I spoke to you while I was still with you, that everything written about me in the Law of Moses and the Prophets and the Psalms must be fulfilled.' Then he opened their minds to understand the Scriptures" (Luke 24:44-45). "Moses and all the Prophets" or "the Law of Moses and the Prophets and the Psalms" are two ways of saying "the whole Old Testament." In other words, Jesus told them that he is found everywhere in the Old Testament.

Notice the source of Jesus' consternation. They did not believe the Scriptures concerning *him*. "O foolish ones, and slow of heart to believe all that the prophets have spoken! Was it not necessary that the Christ should suffer these things and enter into his glory?" (Luke 24:25-26). To put this more bluntly, Jesus *expected* that they would read the Scriptures this way. His thinking could not have been that he was the first to see this in the OT. Otherwise, his expectation would be absurd. Nor was there some kind of implicit thought that only canonically inspired Apostles (which these two were not) were the only ones allowed to interpret the Old Testament with Jesus in mind, because somehow for anyone else to do so would be a dangerous speculative undertaking. No. His expectation was that all of his disciples would have learned by now to read Scripture this way, just as Simeon and Anna had done at his birth when they alluded to Isaiah 8:14-15, 28:16, and 52:8-10 respectively in their blessings of the Christ child (see Luke 2:34, 38).[2]

So, Luke and John both bear witness that this is how Jesus read the Bible. Jesus is either right or wrong about this. There is no middle ground here. We can't fudge with this. We can't play games to skirt around his hermeneutic, pretending with our mouths that we believe it while in practice we do the opposite. I've seen many people do just that. To do this a direct contradiction to Jesus' own teaching. If we do not understand how he can be everywhere in the OT, then the solution is not to deny its truthfulness, but to keep searching until we find the answer. This is what we will begin to see unfolded in the following pages. To get at this, we will first look at several places where the New Testament uses just this kind of interpretation and we will ask ourselves what the implications of this must be.

---

[2] See David W. Pao and Eckhard J. Schnabel, "Luke," in G. K. Beale and D. A. Carson, *Commentary on the New Testament Use of the Old Testament* (Grand Rapids, MI; Nottingham, UK: Baker Academic; Apollos, 2007), 273-74.

Study Questions:

1. What two chapters were cited that show Jesus teaching others how to read the Old Testament?

2. What does the word "hermeneutic" mean?

3. Does Jesus give us a hermeneutic for reading the Bible? If so, what is it?

4. Did Jesus expect that others would interpret the Scripture his way? How do you know?

Part II ‡ NT Passages and Reflections

Some Key NT Passages

THE NT HAS SOME PRETTY AMAZING things to say about Christ in the OT. Speaking of Israel in the wilderness, the Apostle Paul says, "All drank the same spiritual drink. For they drank from the spiritual Rock that followed them, and the Rock was Christ" (1Co 10:4). The Author of Hebrews says of Moses, "He considered the reproach of Christ greater wealth than the treasures of Egypt, for he was looking to the reward" (Heb 11:26). Jude, the half-brother of Jesus says, "I want to remind you, although you once fully knew it, that Jesus, who saved a people out of the land of Egypt, afterward destroyed those who did not believe" (Jude 1:5).[3] The Apostle John says, "Isaiah said

---

[3] As mentioned in the Preface, "Jesus" is a textual variant. "Lord" (*Kurios*) is the other option. Metzger says, "Critical principles seem to

these things because he saw [Christ's] glory and spoke of him" (John 12:41). One more will suffice to make our point. Jesus himself says, "Your father Abraham rejoiced that he would see my day. He saw it and was glad" (John 8:56).

- The Rock was Christ (1Co 10:4)
- Moses considered the reproach of Christ (Heb 11:26)
- Jesus saved a people out of Egypt (Jude 5)
- Isaiah saw Christ's glory (John 12:41)
- Abraham saw Christ's day (John 8:56)

Though the next three chapters will focus on Christ in the OT through prophecy, law, and typology, also vitally important and fundamental is the idea that Christ was himself *in* the OT as a person, not just as an idea. That is what each of these five inspired men teach in one way or another. *Christ* was the Water Israel drank and the Rock that followed them. Moses did not want to disappoint *Christ*. *Jesus* saved the people out of Egypt. Isaiah saw *Christ*. Abraham saw *Jesus'* day. How could this possibly be? It is because

---

require the adoption of 'Iesous [Jesus], which is the best attested reading among Greek and versional witnesses." Bruce Manning Metzger, United Bible Societies, *A Textual Commentary on the Greek New Testament, Second Edition a Companion Volume to the United Bible Societies' Greek New Testament (4th Rev. Ed.)* (London; New York: United Bible Societies, 1994), 657. A similar variant is found in the 1Cointhians 10 passage (vs. 9), above. That one reads "Christ" rather than "Jesus," but "Lord" is the other option. For more, see my sermon on this passage, "I Feel Fine," on Jude 4-8 at www.rbcnc.com.

Christianity teaches that Jesus Christ is both man and God. The human nature of Jesus Christ came into existence in Mary's womb, but the Second Person of the Trinity did not. We will look at this idea much more in later chapters in some very particular and perhaps even shocking ways.

Some Question

For now, I want to finish with a couple of questions. Does your theology of the Second Person of the Trinity allow for him to actually *be in* the OT? If the answer is "yes," then have you been looking for him there?

If the answer is "no," it is important to consider something here. Even if it is "yes," this is still significant. If Jesus is not actually present in the OT, then the apologetic value of these passages becomes worthless. If they Jude and John and the others are saying these things about Jesus, but they are just making them up, then this is no rational argument, much less should it persuade anyone to follow Christ—especially a Jew steeped in the OT. If they were the first to see these things and write about them because Jesus illuminated theirs as the first minds to ever see it, then how could it possibly be true that Moses and Abraham saw Christ, as they tell us they did? This kind of skepticism makes an absurdity of these passages.

But there is another problem. Many have never been taught this hermeneutic. As such, we have a plethora of other ways of reading Scripture out there that miss the point. Many people read the OT as they might read Aesop's Fables to their children: great stories with a moral ending to help us be better people. Others come to the OT as if it were a divinely revealed leadership, coaching, psychology, science, and even dietary and cooking handbook. Still others have become so bored with it that they no longer read it at all. Christ in the OT is a way beyond the moralism, "how-to" manuals, and defeatism. For when he is seen as actually being there with those people, suddenly we can say that those with faith came to him that they might have life (John 5:40). What a profoundly thrilling thought: *People were saved by Jesus and by their faith in Jesus in the OT!*

Study Questions:

1. What five NT passages were cited as teaching that Jesus is in the OT?

2. What does 1Cointhians 10 teach us about Christ?

3. What does Hebrews 11:26 teach us about Moses?

4. Jude 1:5 says that Jesus saved a people out of Egypt. Different copies say it was "the Lord." What is the difference in how you understand "Jesus" vs. "the Lord," and why do you suppose a copiest might be uncomfortable with the original word "Jesus?"

5. Does the idea that Jesus saved people out of Egypt make you uncomfortable? If so, why?

6. What did Isaiah see in John 12:41?

7. What was Abraham rejoicing to see in John 8:56?

Part III ✝ Christ Promised

Christ in Prophecy

Prophecy and the Old Testament

WE WILL NOW BEGIN to look at some specific ways that we see Christ in the OT. The first is Christ as he is *promised*. This takes place through prophecy. Prophecy is a word from God about something that will take place in the future. Prophecy is perhaps the best understood way of seeing Christ in the OT, and it is the easiest to wrap our minds around for that reason (though the idea of prophecy itself is actually a deep mystery). That makes it a good place to start.

Peter says, "God foretold by the mouth of all the prophets, that his Christ would suffer" (Acts 3:18). The word "all" (*panton*) is in the Greek text, and as such it makes for a stunning claim—*all the prophets* talked about Christ. This idea certainly fits with what Jesus himself taught the disciples on the road to Emmaus (see the Introduction). Let's look at a few examples.

Isaiah refers to a "suffering servant." The heart and soul of the prophecies about this Suffering One are found in Isaiah 53. "He was despised and rejected by men; a man of sorrows, and acquainted with grief ... he was despised ... he has borne our griefs and carried our sorrows ... we esteemed him stricken, smitten by God, and afflicted ... he was pierced for our transgressions; he was crushed for our iniquities" (Isa 53:3-5). While the Jews came to interpret this as referring to the nation, it is clear that the prophet has an individual in mind. Thus, the NT cites verses from this chapter in all four Gospels, Acts, Romans, 1 Peter, 1 John and other books.[4] Each time, they say it is fulfilled in the person of Jesus Christ.

---

[4] The passage technically begins in Isaiah 52. So compare:
Isa 52:13 with Acts 3:13
Isa 53:1 with John 12:38 and Rom 10:16
Isa 53:2 with Matt 2:23
Isa 53:3 with Mark 9:12
Isa 53:4 with Matt 8:17 and 1Pe 2:24
Isa 53:4-5 with Rom 4:25
Isa 53:5 with Matt 26:67 and 1Pe 2:25
Isa 53:5-6 with John 1:29
Isa 53:6 with 1Pe 2:25
Isa 53:6-7 with Matt 26:63; 27:12, 14; Mark 10:60-61; 15:4-5; 1Co 5:7; 1Pe 2:23; Rev 5:6, 12; 13:8
Isa 53:7-8 with Acts 8:32-33
Isa 53:8-9 with Matt 26:24; 1Pe 2:22; 1Jn 3:5; Rev 14:5
Isa 53:11 with Rom 5:19
Isa 53:12 with Matt 27:38; Luke 22:37; 23:34; Heb 9:28; 1Pe 2:24

Other prophets talk about Christ's suffering too. In a passage badly misinterpreted by some, *Daniel*, referring to the crucifixion, says that Messiah is "cut off" (Dan 9:26).[5] *Zechariah* talks about Christ being pierced on the cross (Zech 12:10).[6] *David* goes into great detail about the sufferings of Christ. Just one example is Psalm 22 which is perhaps the main text in the OT predicting the specific sufferings of Christ on the cross.[7]

There are many more prophecies as well. *Micah* says he would be born in Bethlehem (Mic 5:2).[8] Isaiah says he would be born of a virgin (Isa 7:14).[9] *Hosea* says he would be called out of Egypt (Hos 11:1).[10] *Jeremiah* talks about the weeping concerning the death of the babies when Herod tried to kill the Christ (Jer 31:15).[11] *Malachi* predicted the messenger John who came to announce the Messiah (Mal 3:1).[12] *Joel* predicted Christ sending the Holy Spirit (Joel 2:28-32).[13] *Moses* foresaw Christ being the greatest prophet (Dt 18:15-19).[14] The Apostle Paul uses *Habakkuk* as a

---

[5] See Luke 21:24.
[6] See John 19:37.
[7] Compare Ps 22:7-8 with Matt 27:39; Mark 15:29; and Luke 23:35-36; Ps 22:8 with Matt 27:42; Ps 22:15 and John 19:28; Ps 22:16-18 with Matt 25:24; Ps 22:18 with Matt 27:35; Mark 15:24; Luke 23:34; John 19:24.
[8] See Matt 2:6; John 7:42.
[9] See cf. Matt 1:23; Luke 1:31; Rev 12:5.
[10] See Matt 2:15.
[11] See Matt 2:18.
[12] See Matt 11:3, 10; Mark 1:2; Luke 1:17, 76; 7:19, 27; John 3:28.
[13] See Acts 2:17-21.
[14] See Matt 17:5; Mark 9:7; John 6:14; Acts 3:22.

summary of the whole work of Christ saying, "I am doing a work in your days that you would not believe if told" (Hab 1:5; cf. Acts 13:41).

These are not the generic, statistically possible predictions of a horoscope, or the mumbling riddles of a Nostradamus that could mean just about anything. They are specific, clear, intelligible, and statistically impossible to occur by chance in the life of a single individual. All of these things were predicted centuries prior to their taking place in history, and the NT teaches us to be looking for Christ through prophecy wherever prophecy is to be found.

What Does Prophecy Do?

Prophecies do at least a couple of things. First, they prove that what took place in the days of Jesus was really and truly from God. "Who is like me," asks the LORD. "Let him proclaim it. Let him declare and set it before me, since I appointed an ancient people. Let them declare what is to come, and what will happen" (Isa 44:7). The point is, only God knows the future.

Second, prophecy is relevant to faith. Now, prophecy does not *create* faith. Jesus records that Abraham said, "They have Moses and the Prophets; let them hear them ... If they do not hear Moses and the Prophets, neither will they be convinced if someone should rise from the dead" (Luke 16:29, 31). Jesus himself said, "If you believed Moses, you would believe me; for he wrote of me" (John 5:46). But prophecies do *strengthen* our faith. "Concerning this salvation, the prophets who prophesied about the grace that was to be yours searched and inquired carefully, inquiring what person or time the Spirit of Christ in them was indicating when he predicted the sufferings of Christ and the subsequent glories" (1Pe 1:10-11).

Perhaps the first and greatest of all these prophecies comes in the Garden of Eden. "I will put enmity between you [Satan] and the woman, and between your offspring and her offspring; he [Christ] shall bruise your head, and you shall bruise his heel" (Gen 3:15). This prophecy has a multilevel fulfillment. At the cross, Satan bruised Christ's heel. At the same time, and through the resurrection and ascension, Christ crushed Satan's head. And very soon, "The God of peace will ... crush Satan under your feet. The grace of our Lord Jesus Christ be with you" (Rom 16:20).

Study Questions:

1. What is Prophecy?

2. What does Acts 3:18 teach us about prophecy?

3. What Prophecies about Christ come to your mind when thinking about the question of prophecy in the OT?

4. What is the content of the first prophecy in the Bible (Gen 3:15)?

Part IV ‡ Christ Patterned

Christ in Typology

What is Typology?

WE HAVE OBSERVED how Christ is seen in the OT through prophecy. Now, we want to look at how he is seen through something called typology. Typology is basically a heavenly eternal archetype (an original that is copied for some purpose) built into redemptive-historical persons, places, or things by God such that they become representative of something else. As an analogy, think of a copper planchet used at a mint. The planchet is literally struck or smashed with the imprint of Abraham Lincoln to become a penny. Or think of an old typewriter where the image of a letter is struck onto a piece of paper. These are "types." Obviously, you can only have a type if the archetype already exists. Christ is the archetype who is "struck" into OT persons, places, and things. This idea is a bit less understood than prophecy, but it is just as important.

The Greek word is *tupos*. It is a rather rare word, but when it is used, it is powerful in meaning. The OT LXX (Septuagint, that is the Greek translation of the Hebrew) has Moses telling the workers of the tabernacle, "See, you shall make them according to the pattern (*tupos*) showed you in the mount" (Ex 25:40). Hebrews comments on this verse saying, "They serve a copy and shadow of heavenly things" (Heb 8:5). The tabernacle had to be replicated exactly as commanded, because it was a visible created shadowy copy of the heavenly invisible sanctuary. The tabernacle was a model, a type, of the heavenly temple. It was not the heavenly temple itself, but a replica that mysteriously brought the people to the heavenly counterpart.

The accompanying drawing (next page) is my own modification of one developed (as far as I can tell) by Geerhardus Vos. It explains how an eternal archetype (A) is brought down into history, first in the form of created shadowy types in the OT era (B). These types both model the preexisting heavenly reality and foreshadow the future coming greater reality. In other words, they point both forward and backward. In the NT (C), the archetype comes down out of heaven and enters into the world of history in the form of the antitype. The antitype is the eternal reality itself coming to us. The greatest antitype is the God-man. Jesus is the archetype become flesh, or to use John's word, the Word made flesh (John 1:1). The

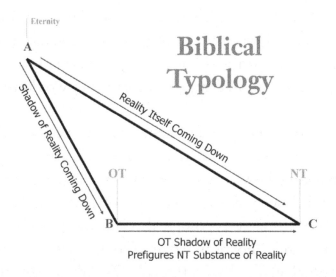

Biblical Typology

Eternity

A

Shadow of Reality Coming Down

Reality Itself Coming Down

OT

NT

B

C

OT Shadow of Reality
Prefigures NT Substance of Reality

Word (which we will look at in a later chapter) is the eternal God, the Second Person of the Trinity.

What are Some Specific Types?

All of the things about the tabernacle were types of the heavenly reality. These included sacrificial animals and the priests who offered them. These animals were types of Christ, for he is the "Lamb of God" who takes away the sin of the world (John 1:29). His was a "better sacrifice" (Heb 9:23). His was a better priesthood (Heb 5:10). He was a better priest, because he was without sin (Heb 4:15). His offering was in a better temple (Matt 12:6), in heaven itself (Heb 9:24), even as he *is* the temple of heaven (John 2:21). Therefore, his was a "better ministry" (Heb 8:6) and a "better covenant" (Heb 7:22), for the old covenant was a type of the new covenant. In these ways and many more, the OT shadows and types were given to point people backward and forward to a heavenly origin and a future fulfillment in someone who would fulfill their purposes.

Sometimes, people in the OT can be viewed as types. The Apostle says that Adam "was a type (*tupos*) of the one who was to come" (Rom 5:14). So, Jesus is called the "second man" (1Co 15:47) and "last Adam" (1Co 15:45). The typological relationship is put this way by Paul, "For as in Adam all die, so also in Christ shall all be made alive" (1Co 15:22). Adam's son Abel was a type. Abel's death was a sacrifice likened to Jesus' own sacrifice which is "better" (Heb 12:24). So, Jesus is a greater Abel, as both were put to death for their righteousness. Jesus says, "They repented at the preaching of Jonah, and behold, something greater than Jonah is here" (Matt 12:41), and adds that the Queen of Sheba "came from the ends of the earth to hear the wisdom of Solomon, and behold, something greater than Solomon is here" (Matt 12:42). Jesus is a greater preacher who has a greater sign (three days in the earth) than Jonah, and who is full of greater wisdom than Solomon. All these men are thus viewed as types of Christ in these ways.

Things and events can also be viewed typologically. Christ says he is the manna that comes down from heaven (John 6:51). Manna in the OT was a physical substance that miraculously fell from heaven and the people ate it in the wilderness for forty years. Peter tells us, Christian baptism is said to correspond (*antitupos*) to the Flood-baptism (1Pe 3:20-21). So, the great Flood becomes a model of our baptism. Paul says, "I do not want you to be unaware, brothers, that our fathers were all under the cloud, and all passed through the sea, and all were baptized into Moses in the cloud and in the sea, and all ate the same spiritual food, and all drank the same spiritual drink. For they drank from the spiritual Rock that followed them, and the Rock was Christ" (1Co 10:1-4). A couple of verses later he adds that the many events of the exodus "took place as examples (*tupos*) for us, that we might not desire evil as they did" (1Co 10:6). This last type is ethical in nature, yet it is still rooted in Christ: "We must not put Christ to the test, as some of them did" (1Co 10:9).

You should understand from these many examples that seeing Christ in typology is more complicated than making some arbitrary and forced connections as some have done. A good example of finding a wrong type can be found in the early church where it was common to see the scarlet thread of Rahab as a type of Christ's blood—because it was red. This is wrong because there is no immediately recognizable correspondence between Rahab's thread and Christ's blood.

You can think of this philosophically to help you understand it. Types are related via their *substances* (sanctuary to sanctuary, blood to blood, water to water, circumcision to circumcision, wisdom to wisdom, three to three, man to Man, grumbling to grumbling),[15] rather than by their *accidents* (the thread and blood both happen to be "red").[16] While not always easy to identify proper types or to apply them correctly, nevertheless, by understanding the simple principles of lesser-greater relationships in historical persons, places, or things that are organically related through their substances, you can and need to be reading the OT through this lens. For in it is contained all the shadowy patterns of things to come, things which, in one way or another, find their fulfillment in Jesus Christ.

---

[15] Hence, the tabernacle (*sanctuary*) to the heavenly temple (*sanctuary*); the *blood* of an animal sacrifice to the *blood* of Christ's sacrifice; the *water* of the great Flood to the *water* of baptism; the *circumcision* of the foreskin to the *circumcision* of the heart; Solomon's *wisdom* to Christ's *wisdom*; and so on. It is curious that the NT creates types through metaphor such that the sacrifice of a lamb becomes the sacrifice of Jesus the Lamb of God. Though it is a metaphor, nevertheless, the substance (i.e. a lamb) is the same.

[16] An "accident" is something that is not essential to the substance. In the case of thread, red is only one of many possible colors. The same is true of blood, as some creatures have blood that is not red.

Study Questions:

1. Define "typology."

2. What kinds of things can be "types" in Scripture?

3. List at least three passages in the NT that cite an OT type.

4. How might typology be similar to prophecy?

5. Why is typology important to a study of Christ in the OT?

6. List some specific OT types that Jesus fulfills.

Part III ‡ Christ Patterned

Christ in the Law

Understanding the Law

ONE OF THE CHIEF CONCERNS of the OT is to make sure that God's people know about righteousness and morality. Righteousness and morality come to us through *law*. I am a Reformed Christian. Many Reformed people hold to things called confessions of faith. These were how the Protestants formally differentiated themselves from Roman Catholics at the beginning of the Reformation. Confessions set up positive, robust statements of what a group believes about the Bible.

My own Confession teaches that the law of God can be divided into three parts: moral, civil, and ceremonial (*London Baptist Confession* 19.3-4). The moral law is summarized in the Ten Commandments, and the other two kinds of law take up much of Exodus, Leviticus, and Deuteronomy. Now is not the time to get into how these distinctions work, other than to say that in the last section we saw some examples of how ceremonial law (i.e. sacrifices, temples, etc.) are fulfilled in Christ via typology. In this section of *Christ Patterned*, I want to focus on how Christ is seen in, especially, the moral law.

The first thing I want to take notice of is that Christ himself was the Giver of the Commandments to Moses. Both Stephen and Paul say that the Law was put into effect through angels (Acts 7:53; Gal 3:19; cf. Dt 33:2 LXX[17]). But Paul adds something interesting. He says that there was an intermediary here. "An intermediary implies more than one, but God is one" (Gal 3:20). Since angels and God are the only two beings mentioned, it would seem that the intermediary is *between them*. If so, this would mean that Moses can't be in mind because, as a man, he is below angels (for now; cf. Ps 8:5).[18] That is, he would mediate between humans and God, not angels and God.

---

[17] Michael Heiser has a short summary of the differences between the LXX and the Hebrew text. See Michael Heiser, "Why Use the Septuagint," *LogosTalk* (Dec 2007), https://blog.logos.com/2007/12/why_use_the_septuagint/, last accessed 11-3-2019.

[18] For the difficulties on this mediator being Moses see F. F. Bruce, *The Epistle to the Galatians: a Commentary on the Greek Text*, New International Greek Testament Commentary (Grand Rapids, MI: W.B. Eerdmans Pub. Co., 1982), 175-80.

This otherwise inexplicable verse is cleared up if God is somehow the intermediary. This is possible given that in the Godhead there is both unity and *plurality*. I believe the intermediary he is talking about is Christ himself, as he is found in the figure of the Angel of the LORD.[19] We will look at this Angel later. For now, it is enough to say that as the Giver of the law, Christ would thus be in the OT in a profound way. This is why, if I were able to create my own red-letter edition of the Bible, the entire Bible would be in red letters, *especially* the OT law.

The Sermon on the Mount

This becomes important when considering Christ and the Law from another viewpoint. This is the vista that he himself shows us in his Sermon on the Mount. Before preaching the greatest sermon ever on the moral law, Jesus begins by saying, "Do not think that I have come to abolish the Law or the Prophets; I have not come to abolish them but to fulfill them" (Matt 5:17). Up to this point in Matthew's book, every time the word "fulfill" has been used, it has meant that Jesus fulfills something from the OT (Matt 1:22; 2:5; 15, 17, 23 etc.), especially a prophecy or a type. In one of these instances, he is baptized in order

---

[19] See Michael S. Heiser, *The Unseen Realm: Recovering the Supernatural Worldview of the Bible*, First Edition (Bellingham, WA: Lexham Press, 2015), 166-67.

to "fulfill all righteousness" (Matt 3:15). There is a typological aspect to this fulfillment,[20] but it is more even than that. According to Deuteronomy 6:25, "righteousness" is directly linked to obeying the law. "And it will be righteousness for us, if we are careful to do all this commandment before the LORD our God, as he has commanded us." In Matthew's Gospel, it refers to good works or obedience (Matt 3:15; 5:10, 20; 6:1; 21:32).[21]

Many people have been deeply confused about what Jesus is doing in the Sermon on the Mount. Many think he is abolishing the law, overthrowing the OT law, intensifying old law, or putting "love" in as the great new law. Some even think he is a different god than the God of the OT, which is why understanding that he was the original Lawgiver is so important. None of those things are true.[22] What Jesus is doing is teaching people:

---

[20] See my book *Waters of Creation: A Biblical-Theological Study of Baptism* (Erie, Co: Waters of Creation Pub., 2009), 13-23, where Jesus is the New Moses, fleeing to Egypt when someone tries to kill all the babies 2 and under (Matt 2), is baptized through the waters (Matt 3), spends a period of "40" in the wilderness to be tempted (Matt 4), and goes up on a mountain to give the Law (Matt 5-7).

[21] See Michael Goulder, *Midrash and Lection in Matthew: The Speaker's Lectures in Biblical Studies, 1969-71* (London: SPCK, 1974), 262 and also my Waters of Creation, 11-12.

[22] See especially Greg Welty, "Eschatological Fulfillment and the Confirmation of Mosaic Law," last accessed 11-5-2019; William Hendriksen and Simon J. Kistemaker, *Exposition of the Gospel According to Matthew*, vol. 9, New Testament Commentary (Grand Rapids: Baker Book House, 1953–2001), 288-383, and my sermon series on the Sermon on the Mount at www.rbcnc.com.

1. What the law has always said.
2. The contrast between his and the Pharisees teaching.
3. That no created man can keep the law perfectly.
4. That something more is needed, namely his own fulfilling of it.

How is Christ in the Law?

In other words, ways we find Jesus in the moral law are to see that:

1. He is the original Lawgiver.
2. This Law reflects God's (and therefore Christ's) holy perfect state of being and bliss.
3. The Law needs to be kept perfectly in order to inherit eternal life (this is the idea of the Covenant of Works); Christ's sinlessness (Heb 4:15) is the fulfillment of the law of God.
4. Christ fulfilled the Law perfectly as a man, so that he might become a greater mediator than the OT prophets and priests (this is the idea of the Covenant of Grace); the Law was a tutor to lead us to Christ (Gal 3:24).

With these lenses, suddenly we can find that reading those most tedious and (some think) boring parts of the OT—the Law of God—can be done in a way that points us beyond those laws to the one who gives them meaning by giving us life through faith in his law-keeping done on our behalf. It ought to make

us profoundly grateful people that God does not require our own perfect obedience in order to have eternal life, while ironically, through this new life and the
Holy Spirit, he creates in us new desires to keep and
obey this very law—the law that was not abolished or
passed away—that once held us captive to Satan
through sin.

Study Questions:

1. What are the three divisions of "law?"

2. What was said about the intermediary between God and angels (Gal 3:20)?

3. Jesus said he came to "fulfill" the law (Matt 5:17). What does "fulfill" mean?

4. The chapter listed four things that show us "the way we find Jesus in the moral law." What are they?

Part V ‡ Christ Present

The Angel of the LORD

Preface to Part V

IN THE NEXT MANY SECTIONS we will turn our attention away from Christ in the OT as he is found in
more general ways like prophecy, types, and law, and
towards Christ as he is literally present in the OT as a
person or figure in Israel's life and history. I will do
this first, by looking at a particular individual that
Geerhardus Vos calls, "The most important and char-
acteristic form of revelation in the patriarchal period."[23] Then I will turn our attention to various
words that came to be understood by Jews (at least for
a time) and early Christians that were, for lack of a
better term, *hypostatically* linked to this individual in
the Old Testament.

---

[23] Geerhardus Vos, *Biblical Theology* (Grand Rapids, MI: Eerdmans,
1977), 72.

The individual in mind here is the Angel of the LORD. Let's return to this idea of Jude that "Jesus saved a people out of Egypt." Where does he get this from? Did he just make it up? No. Instead, it comes from places like Exodus 23:20-21. "Behold, I send an Angel before you to guard you on the way and to bring you to the place that I have prepared. Pay careful attention to him and obey his voice; do not rebel against him, for he will not pardon your transgression, for my name is in him."[24] Let's begin to unpack this a bit.

"The Angel of the LORD" appears with this exact title many times in the OT. He comes explicitly to Hagar (Gen 16:7ff), Abraham (Gen 22:11ff), Moses (Ex 3:2ff), Balaam (Num 22:22ff), Israel (Jdg 2:1ff), Gideon (Jdg 6:21ff), Manoah (Jdg 13:3ff), Elijah (1Kg 19:7ff), Zechariah (Zech 1:11ff), and others. Perhaps the most important (and least remembered) is his first appearance to Moses.

The Burning Bush

The Angel appears to Moses in the Burning Bush. We need to look carefully at the language. "And the Angel of the LORD appeared to him in a flame of fire out of the midst of a bush" (Ex 3:2). There is an angel

---

[24] I will be capitalizing the ESV's lower case "angel."

in the fire (the fire is an image of the Holy Spirit).[25] Who is he? After Moses turns aside to look at this amazing sight (vs. 3) it says, "When the LORD saw that he turned aside to see, God called to him out of the bush" (vs. 4). Here then, the angel is called both *LORD* (Yahweh) and *God* (Elohim). In other words, this is The Angel of the LORD!

What is said here is very similar to what it says after he tells Moses to take his sandals off because the ground is holy (vs. 5). The Angel of the LORD, still speaking, says, "I am the God of your father, the God of Abraham, the God of Isaac, and the God of Jacob." And Moses hid his face for he "was afraid to look at God" (vs. 6). He was afraid to look at God because he could see God in some sense, that is the Angel of God. After a short conversation, Moses asks the Angel of the LORD his name. The Angel says to call him "I AM WHO I AM" (vs. 14) and "Yahweh, the God of your fathers" (vs. 15). Many people have not recognized that all of this is the Angel speaking from the bush, and thus they default to the abstract word "theophany" when trying to explain it. In reality this is the same person who calls himself "I AM" throughout the Gospel of John. In taking this title upon himself, Jesus is claiming to be the Angel in the bush, the very God of Israel.

---

[25] See Meredith Kline, *Images of the Spirit* (Eugene, OR: Wipf & Stock, 1999), 17-20, 72-73.

Gideon

A second story that shows us this interaction between the Angel and the name of God takes place with Gideon. It begins, "Now the angel of the LORD came and sat under the terebinth at Ophrah ... while ... Gideon was beating out wheat in the winepress" (Jdg 6:11). Notice the very physical language here, exactly what we would expect if it were an angel coming to talk to someone.

"And the Angel of the LORD appeared to him and said to him, 'The LORD [Yahweh] is with you, O mighty man of valor.' And Gideon said to him, 'Please, sir, if the LORD is with us, why then has all this happened to us? And where are all his wonderful deeds that our fathers recounted to us, saying, 'Did not the LORD bring us up from Egypt?' But now the LORD has forsaken us and given us into the hand of Midian'" (12-13). Remember when we talked a moment ago about the Angel bringing the people out of Egypt? The same idea is being presented again here.

The next verse is critical. Do not miss it. "And the LORD turned to him and said, 'Go in this might of yours and save Israel from the hand of Midian; do not I send you?'" (14). Here, it explicitly calls the Angel of the LORD "Yahweh," for there is no one else here but these two people. But Gideon did not know it yet. "He said to him, 'Please, Lord [Adonai], how can I save Israel? Behold, my clan is the weakest in Manasseh, and I am the least in my father's house.' And the LORD said to him, 'But I will be with you, and you shall strike the Midianites as one man'" (15-16). Gideon now seems to understand that someone important is talking to him. But who?

"And he said to him, 'If now I have found favor in your eyes, then show me a sign that it is you who speak with me. Please do not depart from here until I come to you and bring out my present and set it before you.' And he said, 'I will stay till you return.' So Gideon went into his house and prepared a young goat and unleavened cakes from an ephah of flour. The meat he put in a basket, and the broth he put in a pot, and brought them to him under the terebinth and presented them. And the angel of God said to him, 'Take the meat and the unleavened cakes, and put them on this rock, and pour the broth over them.' And he did so. Then the angel of the LORD reached out the tip of the staff that was in his hand and touched the meat and the unleavened cakes. And fire sprang up from the rock and consumed the meat and the unleavened cakes. And the angel of the LORD vanished from his sight" (17-21).

Now Gideon understands: "Then Gideon perceived that he was the Angel of the LORD. And Gideon said, 'Alas, O Lord GOD [Adonai Yahweh]! For now I have seen the Angel of the LORD face to face'"

(22). This story does something that, if you begin looking, you will see happening all over the early books of the Bible. Yahweh and the Angel of Yahweh are interchangeable terms, even while Yahweh and the Angel are not interchangeable. In other words, the Angel is both God and not God, or to put it in NT terms, the Angel is God but not the Father; he is the Son of God.

Someone might ask, how could the Angel *be* Yahweh? The Angel of the LORD is Yahweh's messenger, for angels are messengers. In this way, he is distinct from Yahweh (the Father). Delivering messages is the function of an angel. But the term "angel" only speaks to a function. It does not necessarily describe a being's ontology (his DNA, so to speak). Christians understand that God is both One and Three. The idea comes from the Old Testament. This is made clearer by a couple of other passages.

The Angel of the Name

The first returns us to Exodus 23:20-21. "Behold, I send an Angel before you to guard you on the way and to bring you to the place that I have prepared. Pay careful attention to him and obey his voice; do not rebel against him, for he will not pardon your transgression, for my name is in him." Who is speaking here? My opinion is that the Angel of the

LORD is speaking on behalf of Yahweh in heaven (the is the Father's messenger) about the Angel of the LORD; or to put it into NT parlance, the Son is speaking on behalf of the Father about the Son. This is exactly what we see Jesus doing in the NT as well (cf. John 5:20-23; 10:34-38; etc.), as he again identifies himself with this OT Person.

A parallel passage to look at is Judges 2:1-5. It helps inform the previous text. "Now the Angel of the LORD went up from Gilgal to Bochim. And he said, 'I brought you up from Egypt and brought you into the land that I swore to give to your fathers. I said, 'I will never break my covenant with you, and you shall make no covenant with the inhabitants of this land; you shall break down their altars.' But you have not obeyed my voice. What is this you have done? So now I say, I will not drive them out before you, but they shall become thorns in your sides, and their gods shall be a snare to you.' As soon as the angel of the LORD spoke these words to all the people of Israel, the people lifted up their voices and wept. And they called the name of that place Bochim. And they sacrificed there to the LORD."

Notice two things. First, they did not obey his voice, though as we saw in Exodus 22:21, this is what they were commanded to do. Second, the Angel of the LORD is the one who covenanted with Israel. This is because the Angel is the covenant God of Israel. I think most people think much too generically about the covenant making "God," rather than the Second Person of the Trinity who is the intermediary. Yet here it is, right in the Bible.

Jacob

We see the Angel of the LORD being called "God" (*elohim*) other times besides the burning bush. For example, at Bethel it says, "The Angel of God said to me [Jacob] in the dream ... 'I am the God of Bethel'" (Gen 31:11-12). Later, Jacob blesses Joseph and says, "The God before whom my fathers Abraham and Isaac walked, the God who has been my shepherd all my life long to this day, the angel who has redeemed me from all evil, bless the boys" (Gen 48:15-16). Of this passage Calvin says, "It is necessary that Christ should be here meant, who does not bear in vain the title of Angel ... he was always the bond of connection between God and man, and ... For there was always so wide a distance between God and men, that, without a mediator, there could be no communication."[26]

In light of the "saving of people out of Egypt" (Jude 5), the "bringing you to the place" (Ex 23:20), and the "bringing us up from Egypt" (Jdg 6:15) that

---

[26] Genesis 48:16. See John Calvin and John King, *Commentary on the First Book of Moses Called Genesis*, vol. 2 (Bellingham, WA: Logos Bible Software, 2010), 429. Also, see especially the second volume in this series by Peter Allix.

are all said of either Jesus or the Angel of the LORD, it is curious to note that Jacob says, "The angel ... has redeemed me from all evil" (Gen 48:16). Though he is living prior to the exodus, the idea of deliverance or rescuing or saving is the same. In fact, the word used (*go'el*) means a kinsman redeemer.

Joshua

The Angel of the LORD is called Yahweh, God, and I AM, among other names that we normally associated in our minds only with "God" (the one being) or perhaps with the Father. He also covenants with Israel, fights for his people, redeems them from slavery, forgives sin, and must be obeyed. Perhaps one final thing should be mentioned here.

When he shows himself to Joshua as the commander of the army of the LORD, he tells Joshua the very same thing he told Moses, "Take off your sandals from your feet, for the place where you are standing is holy" (Josh 5:15; cf. Ex 3:5). This was in response to Joshua's "worship" (vs. 14), which the Angel accepted. Now, unless this was actually an evil fallen heavenly being, he would not have accepted worship (cf. Rev 22:9) unless he was God.

Study Questions:

1. What key OT passage was said helps us interpret Jude 5?

2. Who spoke to Moses in the burning bush? What name did he give himself?

3. What common word for God is used to help identify the Angel of the LORD in the Gideon story?

4. Who covenanted with the people at Bochim (Judges 2:1-5)?

5. What common term is used synonymously with "angel" by Jacob?

6. What figure identifies himself as the person in the Burning Bush to Joshua (Josh 5:15)?

Part V ‡ Christ Present

λόγος

The Word of God

The Logos

NOW WE WILL TURN our attention to various words
and ideas that are identified with the Angel in such a
way that they become synonymous with Him. I will
begin with "the Word." The word of God can be understood in two mysteriously united senses. The first
is that of God's *speech*. "Long ago, at many times and
in many ways, God spoke to our fathers by the prophets" (Heb 1:1). These prophets put their words, their
speech, down on paper which became Holy Scripture:
God's word. "They received the word with all eager-
ness, examining the Scriptures daily to see if these
things were so" (Acts 17:11).

The second way the Word of God can be understood is through God's *Son*. "In these last days he has
spoken to us by his Son" (Heb 1:2). He is the Word of
God. "In the beginning was the Word, and the Word

was with God, and the Word was God ... And the word became flesh and dwelt among us" (John 1:1, 14). Many are familiar with the Greek word for "word" here. It is *logos*. But where does John get this idea? Is he just making it up?

Many read John against the backdrop of later Greek Gnosticism. Yet, it is clear that John 1:1ff is a reflection on the OT (Genesis 1:1ff). Also, John is a Jew, and there are Jewish (biblical) roots for seeing a figure in the OT who is called both the Angel and the Word. This figure seems to be both God and yet not God. This fact may be surprising to many readers for the simple reason that modern Judaism is Unitarian. To see plurality in a "Godhead" is, for today's Jew, the ultimate blasphemy. "The LORD our God, the LORD is one" (Dt 6:4). Period.

Many Christians have uncritically adopted this Unitarian view of God in their OT thinking about God, "No one could possibly know about a Second Person in a Godhead from the OT. Only in the NT do we see this." Never mind the Angel. Never mind the implications of a theology that comes out of thin air like a magician pulling a rabbit out of a hat. Never mind that the NT was using the OT to prove this theology, which would have been utterly unconvincing if they were just making it up. So, let's turn our attention to three OT passages in order to see that John is getting the concept from the Scriptures.

Abraham

We will first look at Abram prior to his name becoming Abraham. Genesis 15:1 says, "After these things the word of the LORD came to Abram in a vision" (Gen 15:1). Pause a second to think about this. Words do not come to eyes, but to ears. There are some curious things that happen after this. First, Abram responds to the word of the LORD by calling him "Adonai-Yahweh" ("Lord GOD;" 15:2, 8). It is interesting to note that Adonai is the same term David uses to speak of his "Lord," a Lord who is distinct from another LORD (Yahweh) in Psalm 110:1. To put that more simply, there are three persons in the Psalm verse: Yahweh, Adonai, and David. The NT quotes or alludes to this verse in the Psalm perhaps more than any verse in the OT. Each time it calls this Adonai Jesus and makes him separate from the Father.[27] So Jesus is Adonai, at least in the Psalm.

Going back to Genesis, second, the word of the LORD, "brought him [Abram] outside" (Gen 15:5). Is this purely figurative speech? One thing that is probably true at this point is relevant here. Abram is not yet asleep, for the text makes a point to tell us that he falls into a sleep only later on in the story (Gen 15:12).

---

[27] Matt 22:44; 26:64; Mark 12:36; 14:62; 16:19; Luke 20:42-43; 22:69; Acts 2:34-35; Rom 8:34; 1Co 15:25; Eph 1:20; Col 3:1; Heb 1:3, 13; 8:1; 10:12-13; 12:2.

Third, the word of the LORD is simply called "Yahweh" (Jehovah, LORD; vs. 13). We actually see two Yahweh's later on in the same story (one in heaven, one on earth), in Genesis 19:24, a text that nearly every Church Father said refers to the Father and the Son.[28]

Fourth, the LORD walks through pieces of dead animals. Some might suggest that it was just a smoking pot and a flaming torch that were sort of dancing through the pieces of the animals like some kind of cartoonish personification. But it seems pretty clear that "The LORD" (vs. 13) is the person holding these two objects as he walks through with them.

Jeremiah

A second story is the calling of Jeremiah. It begins by saying, "Now the word of the LORD came to me" (Jer 1:4). The LXX has *logos* here, as it does for most of prophets who have the "word of the LORD" come to them.

---

[28] Justin Martyr, *Dialogue* 127; Pseudo-Ignatius, *Antiochians* 2; Irenaeus, *Against Heresies* 3.6.1; Tertullian, *Against Praxeas* 13; Cyprian, *Against the Jews* 3.33; Novatian, *On the Trinity* 18.15–17; Eusebius, *Ecclesiastical History* 1.2.9; Athanasius, *Discourses Against the Arians* 2.15.13; Hilary of Poitiers, *On the Trinity* 5.16; Gregory Nazianzen, *Oration* 29:17; Basil, *On Prov.* 7:22; Ambrose, *Exposition of the Christian Faith* 1.3.22-23; Chrysostom, *Homily 3*: 2 Tim 1:13-18; Augustine, *Tractates on John* 51.3; Cyril, *Comments on 1 John 1:2*; Socrates Scholasticus, *Ecclesiastical History* 2.30; *Constitutions of the Holy Apostles* 5.20. There were even Jews who were saying this referred to two Yahwehs. See R. Ishmael b. Yosi (170-200 C.E.), Gen 19:24 (*b. Sanh.* 38b or 4:5, V.11 A-C); *Genesis Rabbah* 51.2.

Let's notice three things about the rest of Jeremiah's call. First, Jeremiah responds to the word by saying, "Lord GOD" (Adonai-Yahweh; vs. 6). This is identical to Abraham, except that this time the association with the "word" or *logos* is as "Lord GOD" seems explicit. Second, the text next calls "the word of the LORD," simply "the LORD" (Yahweh; Jer 1:7, 9). "The word of the LORD came to me" (vs. 4) becomes "the LORD said" (vs. 7). Many people miss these subtleties of the text, but the NT authors sure didn't. Putting that another way, it is very possible to take this as saying that the Word of the LORD is the LORD. Third, it says the LORD "put out his hand and touched my mouth" (1:9). Words don't do this. Persons do. This is not anthropomorphic language. It is the Angel of the LORD who is called the Word of God.

Samuel

The third story is the call of Samuel. It begins, "The word of the LORD was rare in those days; there was no frequent vision" (1Sa 3:1). Here we have the word associated with a vision again, and this is common among all the prophets. Then it gives us the strange detail that Eli's eyes had begun to grow dim (vs. 2). This is not referring to his "spiritual" sight. The man was literally going blind. This little detail about Eli seems clearly related to the word coming to the eyes in visions.

But first, the word of the LORD is called Yahweh again (4). As one would expect, he speaks to Samuel (three times). But it tells us that Samuel did not recognize the LORD because "he did not yet know the LORD, and the word of the LORD had not yet been revealed to him" (vs. 7). Finally, to get his attention, "The LORD came and stood, calling as at other times" (vs. 10). Apparently, Eli could not help Samuel figure out who this was because he could not see. I wonder, when you read these kinds of things, is your first impulse to think of Christ or to think that the present author (me and others who have seen these things) are completely stretching it?

John identifies Christ as the Word in many places. For example, he sees a rider on a white horse who is called Faithful and True (Rev 19:11). This rider judges and makes war, thus identifying him with the Captain of the Armies of the LORD, the Angel of the LORD from Joshua 5. But just a couple verses later he says, "He is clothed in a robe dipped in blood, and the name by which he is called is The Word of God" (13).

It is not only John. Hebrews connects this to Jesus. Read the following familiar passage now through the eyes of the OT-NT *logos* theology. "Let us therefore strive to enter that rest, so that no one may fall by the same sort of disobedience. For the word of God is living and active, sharper than any two-edged sword, piercing to the division of soul and of spirit, of joints and of marrow, and discerning the thoughts and intentions of the heart. And no creature is hidden from his sight, but all are naked and exposed to the eyes of him to whom we must give account. Since then we have a great high priest who has passed through the heavens, Jesus, the Son of God, let us hold fast our confession" (Heb 4:11-14). Hebrews directly links the Word of God with Jesus, via the pronouns "him" and "his," rather than what we would expect if this was not a person: "it." The "word of God" in this passage is Christ. Long ago, Athanasius said, "For the Son of God is 'living and active,' and works day by day, and brings about the salvation of all" (Athanasius, *On the Incarnation of the Word* 31.3).[29]

In conclusion, we see the Word of the LORD being called Yahweh by the texts, Adonai by the men, he stands, he touches with hands, he takes someone outside, and he walks through pieces of dead animals. Since the Word of God and the Angel are so closely linked, we can now begin to make sense of how the Word is seen as embodied. Just like other angels that

---

[29] Other Fathers making the same connection include Ambrose (*On Faith* 4.7.74); Origen (*Commentary* John 1.36), John Cassian (*Conferences* 7:13), John of Damascus (*On the Orthodox Faith* 4.13), and Basil the Great (Letter 260.9). See also John Owen, *Exposition of Hebrews* on this passage.

are not anthropomorphisms or literary devices, but real living entities, so also the Word of the LORD is the Angel of the LORD. The Word is an aspect of the power of God which we will turn to in the next section.

Study Questions:

1. What are the two ways "word" can be understood in the Bible?

2. What Greek word does the English term "word" come from (John 1:1)?

3. In what manner did the "Word" come to Abraham (Gen 15:1)?

4. What name for God is equivalent for "Word" in Jeremiah 1:7?

5. What reason is given for Eli not being able to figure out that the Word was talking to Samuel (1 Sam 3:1-2)?

6. What physical thing did the "Word" do in Samuel's presence (1Sa 3:10)?

7. What pronoun is used of the "word of God" in Heb 4:13?

Part V ‡ Christ Present

The Power of God

The Memra

DURING THE TIME of Christ, the OT Scriptures
were translated into the language of Aramaic so that
the people of Jesus' day could understand them. Some
of these were virtual translations, but others were
more like Bibles with study notes. They are all called
Targums. Sometimes the Targums add commentary
while other times they seem to add oral tradition. The
point is always to illumine the meaning of the text.

In Aramaic, the word "*memra*" is the equivalent
of the Greek *logos*. It occurs regularly in the Targums.
According to one scholar, "'Memra is used as a buffer
word, introduced apparently for some theological
purpose, such as to avoid anthropomorphisms, or to
avoid making God the direct object or subject of

actions connected with creation."[30] Or, maybe (and this could be a both/and), it was added because they understood a plurality in a Godhead.

In the Targums, "I have established my covenant between me and you" (Gen 17:7) becomes, "I have established My covenant between my Memra [Word] and you." "They heard the sound/voice of the LORD God" (Gen 3:8) becomes, "They heard the voice of the Memra of the Lord God. " They heard the voice of the word? That sounds strange, unless something else is going on. They even do it in our previous passage with Abram. A Targum on Genesis 15:1 reads, "The word (*pithgama*) of the LORD was with Abram in a prophecy, as follows: 'Do not fear, Abram, my Memra (*memra*) shall be your strength." Notice that there are two Aramaic words used for "word" here. The Targum is essentially separating "words" from a person, deifying the Memra as a kind of Second (good) Power in heaven.

This is coming from monotheistic Jews. This was not Zoroastrian dualism with two equal but opposite gods (one good, one evil), but two good, equal, yet distinct persons of a Godhead. This is the same theological and exegetical reservoir from which John is drawing for his *logos* theology.

---

[30] Kevin Cathcart, Michael Maher, and Martin McNamara, eds., *The Aramaic BibleA: Targum Neofiti 1: Genesis*, trans. Martin McNamara, vol. 1 (Collegeville, MN: The Liturgical Press, 1992), 38.

Two Powers in Heaven

In fact, the rabbis and Jewish philosophers actually called this "two powers." This is their language.[31] For example, Philo (20 BC – c. 50 AD) the Jewish philosopher and historian says, "In the one living and true God there were two supreme and primary powers—goodness and authority; and that by his goodness he had created everything, and by his authority he governed all that he had created" (Philo, *On the Cherubim* 9.27). "The creative power … Moses calls God" (*On Flight and Finding* 97), and "by means of this [creative and eternal] power [called God] the Father, who begot and created all things, did also disperse and arrange them" (*On the Change of Names* 29). Given its

---

[31] The modern ground-breaking study of this is Alan F. Segal, *Two Powers in Heaven: Early Rabbinic Reports about Christianity and Gnosticism* (SJLA 25; Leiden: E. J. Brill, 1977). For a much older treatment, see Peter Allix, *The Judgment of the Ancient Jewish Church Against the Unitarians* (London: R. Chiswell, 1699), 145-157 (we have not reproduced this section of his book as part of this series). Other helpful works include Richard Bauckham, "The Throne of God and the Worship of Jesus," in *The Jewish Roots of Christological Monotheism: Papers from the St. Andrews Conference on the Historical Origins of the Worship of Jesus*, ed. C. Newman, J. Davila, and G. Lewis (Leiden: E. J. Brill, 1999), 43-69; Daniel Boyarin, "The Gospel of the Memra: Jewish Binitarianism and the Prologue to John," *Harvard Theological Review* 94:3 (2001): 243-84; M. J. Edwards, "Justin's Logos and the Word of God," *JECS* 3 (1995): 261-80; Larry Hurtado, "The Binitarian Shape of Early Christian Worship," in *The Jewish Roots of Christological Monotheism: Papers from the St. Andrews Conference on the Historical Origins of the Worship of Jesus* (ed. Carey C. Newman, James R. Davila, and Gladys S. Lewis; Leiden: E. J. Brill, 1999), 187-213; Michael Heiser, *The Unseen Realm*, (Bellingham, WA: Lexham, 2015).

close association with the Word (and as we will see later, Wisdom) from Genesis 1, one of these powers is the *Logos*, which we have already seen is Christ.

Philo was a Jew, not a polytheistic pagan. Though he does not seem to have ever come into contact with Christians, and therefore never became one, he nevertheless writes, "Examine it accurately, and see whether there are really two Gods ... There is one true God only ... and what he here calls God (not 'the God' but 'of God') is his most ancient *logos*" (*On Dreams* 1.228-230). Again, he will say, "No mortal thing could have been formed on the similitude of the supreme Father of the universe, but only after the pattern of the second deity, who is the *logos* of the supreme Being" (*Questions on Genesis* 2.62). Philo was not thinking of the *logos* in terms of "logic" or "reason," or even Torah (law), but in terms of a person.

Thus, he will say, "And even if there be not as yet anyone who is worthy to be called a son of God, nevertheless let him labor earnestly to be adorned according to his first-born word [*logos*], the eldest of his angels, as the great archangel of many names; for he is called, the authority, and the name of God, and the Word [*logos*], and man according to God's image, and he who sees Israel. For even if we are not yet suitable to be called the sons of God, still we may deserve to be called the children of his eternal image, of his most sacred *logos*; for the image of God is his most ancient word [*logos*]" (*Confusion of Tongues* 146-47). He says this right after saying, "For that which is higher than all powers is understood to exceed them, not merely in the fact of its existence. But the power of this being which made and arranged everything is with perfect truth called God, and it contains everything in its bosom, and pervades every portion of the universe" (*Confusion* 137).

Power in the NT and Beyond

"Power" is not a term utilized all that much by NT authors. Nevertheless, it is there. More importantly, it points us directly to Christ. Perhaps the most explicit place is 1 Cointhians 1:24 which says, "To those who are called, both Jews and Greek, Christ the Power of God and the Wisdom of God."[32]

This personification or hypostasis of "power" with Christ is exemplified in many places in both Testaments. For example, "our citizenship is in heaven, and from it we await a Savior, the Lord Jesus Christ, who will transform our lowly body to be like his glorious body, by the power that enables him even to subject all things to himself" (Php 3:20-21).

Moving backwards in time, at his death Jesus says, "I tell you, from now on you will see the Son of Man seated at the right hand of Power and coming on the

---

[32] I am again capitalizing the ESV's lower case "power" and "wisdom," as I will do in later chapters with the other terms.

clouds of heaven" (Matt 26:64).[33] During his healing ministry, "all the crowd sought to touch him, for power came out from him and healed them all" (Luke 6:19).

OT precedent for this can be seen in the highly Christological passage of Psalm 24:9-10. The Hebrew reads, "Lift up your heads, O gates! And lift them up, O ancient doors, that the King of glory may come in" (Ps 24:9). Who is this King of Glory? In the next verse, he is the Lord of Hosts (10). But often, the LXX translates the Lord of Hosts as the Lord of Power (cf. Josh 5:14) or Powers (cf. 2Sa 6:2; Zech 7:4).

Another example is from Isaiah. Paul says, "But he said to me, 'My grace is sufficient for you, for my power is made perfect in weakness.' Therefore, I will boast all the more gladly of my weaknesses, so that the power of Christ may rest upon me" (2Co 12:9). Some have argued that Paul is alluding here to Isaiah, "He gives power to the faint, and to him who has no might he increases strength" (Isa 40:29). If so, he is clearly identifying Isaiah's "power" as Christ.

The Reason for Jewish Unitarianism

As a result of this kind of thinking, we can start to make sense of why so many Jews were actually being convinced by the arguments of the NT and early church of a Second God-Person being right there in

---

[33] The ESV does capitalize "Power" here.

the history of OT peoples. It wasn't coming from Greek philosophy; much less was it being made up. It was coming from the OT, and there was an entire strain of rabbinical teaching that saw a plurality in the Godhead via God's powers. We can still see it to this day, if we know where to look.

This in turn actually becomes perhaps the main reason why Judaism is now Unitarian. Two-powers theology was being utilized all over the place by the NT. What made this different from others like Philo is that Jews were converting left and right to Christianity. Combine this with the destruction of their temple and centralized religion in 70 A.D., and you can see how such problems could cause the Rabbis to declare two-powers theology heresy sometime in the late first to early second centuries (see Segal, n. 31). Judaism has been Unitarian in outlook ever since.

We've only begun to see this kind of "power" thinking as related to Christ the term *Logos*, but Philo hints at more. We will turn to one of these that he names explicitly next: The Name of God.

Study Questions:

1. What Aramaic term is equivalent to the Greek word "logos" and the English term "word?"

2. What phrase did some Jewish Rabbis and Philosophers use to explain God's word or *logos*?

3. What Jewish historian/philosopher contemporary with Christ, but who never heard of Jesus Christ, puts Word, Angel, Son, Image, Name, and Firstborn together?

4. What was proposed as the chief reason that Judaism is now a Unitarian religion incapable of seeing a plurality in a Godhead?

Part V ✠ Christ Present

The Name of God

Making a Name

NAMES ARE VERY IMPORTANT things in the Bible, and God has many of them: Yahweh/Jehovah, El, Elyon, and many, many more. Each name reveals something about God's character and attributes: El Shaddai (God of the Mountain), El Roi (God Who Sees), El Elyon (God Almighty), El Olam (Everlasting God), El Channun (Gracious God), Immanuel (God With Us), etc. But though he has many names, very early on in the Bible, God sets in motion a plan in response to the people at Babel who want "to make a name" for themselves (Gen 11:4). This plan is essentially to make (to glorify) a Name for himself.

"Name" is the word *shem* in Hebrew. Shem also happens to be one of the sons of Noah. Curiously, it is through Shem that the promised Seed will come (Gen 9:26-27). This is a promise that goes all the way back to Genesis 3:15 when God promised that Eve would have a Seed who would crush the head of the serpent. How might this work? Let's return to the idea of the Angel of the LORD.

Names of the Angel of the LORD

My favorite name for the Angel of the LORD in Jewish literature has to be Metatron (as opposed to Megatron, the evil leader of the Decepticons). No one quite knows its origin. Sometimes called "lesser Yahweh," some have suggested the possibility that the "him" in Ex 23:21 ("because my name is within *him* [the Angel])" refers to Metatron, where the *ttr* in the word comes from *tetra*, the word for "four" in Greek, and a shorthand for the Tetragrammaton word YHWH.[34]

With such luminary Protestants as Calvin, Isaac Watts, Charles Spurgeon, and Matthew Henry as well as OT scholars like Meredith Kline,[35] many through the centuries have suggested that a biblical proper name for this Angel is Michael. Michael is an archangel (Jude 9; Rev 12:7) of the heavenly council.[36] This

---

[34] See Andrei A. Orlov, *The Etymology of the Name 'Metatron,"* in *The Enoch-Metatron Tradition* (TSAJ, 107; Tuebiingen: Mohr-Sieback, 2005). An excerpt is here. See point #7: last accessed 8-14-2014.

[35] Calvin, Daniel 10:13; Watts, *The Glory of Christ as God-Man* 3.5; Spurgeon, The Angelic Life sermon 842; Kline, Kingdom Prologue Lecture 22.

[36] Also called the "divine council" (Ps 82:1), this is the group of heavenly beings (*elohim*) variously called the "sons of God" (Job 38:7; Ps 82:6) or "watchers" (Dan 4:17) who administer the affairs of the cosmos. Also 1Kg 22:13-23; Isa 6:1-9; Dan 7:9-14; etc. See Michael S. Heiser, "Divine Council," in Tremper Longman III and Peter Enns,

council includes the heavenly angelic princes of Greece and Persia (Dan 10:20) and other "sons of God" (Ps 82:1). In Daniel, he is called "Michael your [Israel's] prince" (Dan 10:21) and "the great prince" (12:1).

Michael is a proper name. The name means "who is like God" (*mi-ka'el*). It can be either a statement or a question. If it is a statement, then it may point toward the direction that Michael is one who is like God. If it is a question, it might be read in light of Exodus 15:11, "Who is like you, O LORD among the gods (*mi-kamokah ba'elim yhwh*) ... doing wonders (*pele'*)?"

There are a couple of lines to pursue here. First, let's look at the anatomy of this phrase in Exodus. When the Angel of the LORD appeared to Samson's mother and father, and he was asked his name, the Angel responded, "Why do you ask my name, seeing it is *Wonderful*?" (Jdg 13:18). This is similar to "doing wonders." It is interesting that the Angel phrases his response in the form of a question, just like the name Michael may be. This is of further interest in light of Isaiah 9:6 which predicts of the Messiah, "His name shall be called Wonderful (*pele'*), Counselor." Curiously, the LXX of this verse reads, "His name is called the Angel of the great council," and many Fathers

---

eds., *Dictionary of the Old Testament: Wisdom, Poetry & Writings* (Downers Grove, IL; Nottingham, England: IVP Academic; Inter-Varsity Press, 2008).

used the LXX here to prove that Jesus was the Angel of the LORD before coming as a man. Thus, we can see from Ex 15:11, Jdg 13:18, and Isa 9:6 all have the idea of "wonder" in the name.

A second line of thought revolves around the two times that the phrase "The LORD rebuke you" is found. In the first, "The Angel of the LORD" speaks these words to Satan (Zech 3:1-2). In this passage, the "Angel of the LORD" and "Yahweh" are interchangeable. In the second, it is Michael who speaks these words to Satan (Jude 9), and this seems a deliberate echo, if not a quote, from Zechariah.[37]

Along these lines, we think about the only (other?) archangel mentioned in Scripture. The Apostle says, "For the Lord himself will descend from heaven with a cry of command, with the voice of an archangel, and with the sound of the trumpet of God. And the dead in Christ will rise first" (1Th 4:16). While it could be that the Lord Jesus is distinct from the archangel here, it could also be that he is the Archangel. Consider this amazing verse in light of something Jesus said, "Truly, truly, I say to you, an hour is coming, and is now here, when the dead will hear the voice of the Son of God, and those who hear will live." (John 5:25).

---

[37] See Richard J. Bauckham, *2 Peter, Jude*, vol. 50, Word Biblical Commentary (Dallas: Word, Incorporated, 1998), 65. Bauckham and many others do not take the view that Michael is the Angel.

With such similarities, it should be at least noted that while Michael is said to be "the great prince in charge of [God's] people" (Dan 12:1) and "[Israel's] prince" (Dan 10:21), in an earlier passage Israel is said to be Yahweh's, that is the Angel of the LORD's portion in Deuteronomy 32:9. While the text simply says "Yawheh," it is clear from the context that this cannot refer to the Father, for it is the Father (the Most High, Dt 32:7) who is dividing the nations among the "sons of God" (8), and the LORD's portion is Israel (9). Therefore, the Yahweh is vs. 9 is not the Father, but the Son of God.

Hence, the LORD in Deuteronomy is most likely Michael in Daniel. This would make perfect sense if Michael is the proper name for the Angel, but it is difficult to reconcile if there are somehow two angels in charge of Israel. In the rest of this chapter, I want to focus on how the Name of the LORD actually becomes personified in much the same way that the Word does.

Name Personified

The NT refers to "names that are named" (Eph 1:21). In the verse, "names" is akin to "authorities," "powers," and "dominions," all titles of supernatural entities. So, these entities are actually called "names." Often, in the same verse, we are commanded to praise "the LORD" and then the "Name of the LORD" (Ps 113:1; 135:1; etc.). Similarly, we give thanks "to the LORD," and also to the "Name of the LORD" (Ps 122:4). People are to fear "the LORD," but also "the Name of the LORD" (Isa 59:19). The LORD is great, but then the Name is great (Jer 10:6). The same goes for trusting (Isa 50:10), loving (Isa 56:6), and glorifying (Isa 24:15). Normally we praise, thank, fear, trust, and love *people*. Therefore, the name of the LORD takes on a kind of identity all his own in these verses.[38]

Psalm 75:1 has the Psalmist rejoicing because God's Name is near. Conversely, Isaiah 30:27 says, "Behold, the Name of the LORD comes from afar, burning with his anger, and in thick rising smoke; his lips are full of fury, and his tongue is like a devouring fire." Here "anger" and "fury" are attributed to the Name. This has led scholars to summarize that, "God's name has become virtually an independent entity, separate from God, i.e. a hypostasis."[39] In my opinion, "Name" in these places should therefore be capitalized, as it often is in the great hymns of the faith. For example,

---

[38] In the grammar, "of the LORD" is a prepositional phrase. This means that the subject of "the Name of the LORD" is not "the LORD" but "the Name." "Of the LORD" modifies The Name. I have capitalized the ESV's "name."

[39] H. B. Huffmon, "Name," ed. Karel van der Toorn, Bob Becking, and Pieter W. van der Horst, *Dictionary of Deities and Demons in the Bible* (Leiden; Boston; Köln; Grand Rapids, MI; Cambridge: Brill; Eerdmans, 1999), 611.

Immortal, invisible, God only wise,
In light inaccessible hid from our eyes,
Most blessed, most glorious, the Ancient of Days,
Almighty, victorious, thy great Name we praise.

We can see this from the NT. Nehemiah 9:5 says, "Blessed be your glorious Name, which is exalted above all blessing and praise." The NT takes this passage and interprets it for us saying, "God has highly exalted him [Jesus] and bestowed on him the name that is above every name, so that at the name of Jesus every knee should bow, in heaven and on earth and under the earth" (Php 2:9-10).

All of this is what Exodus 23:21 means when it says of the Angel, "My Name is in him." "Name" becomes a way to have a piece of yourself in someone else, like when a father names his son after himself, thus calling him Jr. He biologically sires his son and then gives him the same name. The difference is, the Second Person of the Trinity is "eternally begotten" and very God of very God.

Place of the Name

Finally, Moses says, "You shall seek the place that the LORD your God will choose out of all your tribes to put his Name and make his habitation there" (Dt 12:5). In the OT, this habitation was in the temple in Jerusalem. As we saw earlier, Jesus now says he is the Temple (John 2:21). When you see "the Name of the LORD," think about capitalizing it in your mind. Read it with Christ as the embodiment. For "Jesus" means "Ya [God] Saves" and "Christ" means "Anointed One." His name is Emmanuel—God with us. He is the place where atonement and life with God is carried out. He is the place of God's Name.

Study Questions:

1. What do God's names reveal about himself?

2. What have some Christians believed is a proper name for the Angel of the LORD? What does this name mean?

3. The terms "wonders" or "wonderful" are used of the Angel in what three passages as discussed in the chapter?

4. What are heavenly beings called in Ephesians 1:21?

5. What emotions are attributed to the Name by Isaiah?

6. What OT passage does Philippians 2:9-10 reflect upon?

7. In Deuteronomy 12:5, what is the place of God's Name?

Part V ‡ Christ Present

The Wisdom of God

Wisdom

THE NT ENCOURAGES US, "To reach all the riches of full assurance of understanding and the knowledge of God's mystery, which is Christ, in whom are hidden all the treasures of wisdom and knowledge" (Col 2:2-3). Paul says this because Jesus himself said (in a passage we saw on typology), "The queen of the South will rise up at the judgment with this generation and condemn it, for she came from the ends of the earth to hear the wisdom of Solomon, and behold, something greater than Solomon is here" (Matt 12:42).

Solomon was of course known for his wisdom. God basically gave him one wish where he could have anything he wanted. "Ask what I shall give you" (2Ch 1:7). "Give me now wisdom and knowledge" (10), was his answer. God (presumably the Angel) was very pleased with this response, because Solomon did not ask for "possessions, wealth, honor, or the life of those who hate you … or even long life" (11), or might I add, like I probably would have done, a thousand more wishes(!). So, "God gave Solomon wisdom and understanding beyond measure ... Solomon's wisdom surpassed the wisdom of all the people of the east and all the wisdom of Egypt ... And people of all nations came to hear the wisdom of Solomon, and from all the kings of the earth, who had heard of his wisdom" (1Kg 4:29, 30, 34). Somehow Christ is greater than this, but how?

A common way of answering this question is by demonstrating how wise Jesus actually was. Or, to put it another way, by going to the NT. Throughout his ministry, he was constantly outsmarting the Pharisees or teaching the Scripture with authority that no one else had. This is all true, of course, and necessary to know; but I have something else in mind here. This is a book on Christ in the Old Testament. So how might Christ be the Wisdom of God *in the* OT?

Wisdom at Creation

Let us remember that Solomon was the author of most of the Proverbs, including Proverbs 8. The end of this chapter has a rather extended and fascinating claim made by Wisdom:

> [22] The LORD possessed me at the beginning of his work, the first of his acts of old.

23 Ages ago I was set up, at the first, before the beginning of the earth.

24 When there were no depths I was brought forth, when there were no springs abounding with water.

25 Before the mountains had been shaped, before the hills, I was brought forth,

26 before he had made the earth with its fields, or the first of the dust of the world.

27 When he established the heavens, I was there; when he drew a circle on the face of the deep,

28 when he made firm the skies above, when he established the fountains of the deep,

29 when he assigned to the sea its limit, so that the waters might not transgress his command, when he marked out the foundations of the earth,

30 then I was beside him, like a master workman, and I was daily his delight, rejoicing before him always,

31 rejoicing in his inhabited world and delighting in the children of man.

(Prov 8:22-31)

Clearly, this does not refer to Solomon. But it does seem to refer to someone, that is, to *a person*.

There are many fascinating correlations here to the creation episode of Genesis 1. Several words are found in both passages: *beginning, the deep, water, sea, heaven, earth*, and *man*. The Targum's interpretation of Genesis 1:1 seems to have Proverbs 8 in mind. "From the beginning with wisdom the Memra of the Lord created and perfected the heavens and the earth." Notice the link bet-ween the word ("Memra") and the wisdom of God. Almost all of the words we have been considering in these last chapters are related very closely in the texts, because they are all talking about the same Person. Combining the power and wisdom of God at creation, the Apostle says, "Christ [is] the power of God and the wisdom of God" (1Co 1:24).

Wisdom, the Law, and the Angel

Part of being wise is being able to properly discern and give proper judgment about God's law. In 2 Samuel it says, "But my lord the king is like the angel of God;[40] do therefore what seems good to you" (2Sa 19:27). The worldview here is important. It reflects the idea that God gave 70 heavenly sons of God to rule over the nations (Dt 32:7-8). They were supposed to rule with wisdom and justice. But they failed miserably (Ps 82:1-5). However, the Angel of the LORD does rule over Israel with wisdom and justice, and as the human king is the complement to the Angel on earth, he is likened to the Angel in heaven. David VanDrunen writes, "When human beings execute justice properly, Scripture sometimes likens them to

---

[40] This verse has the definite article "the." This is different from the two 2 Samuel verses listed below. However, the conceptual ideas are similar in that they surround wisdom and judgments. Therefore, the ESV has "the Angel..." in all three cases.

angels. In addition to Psalm 8:5-6, in which the exercise of dominion places humans 'a little lower' than the angels, 2 Samuel 14:17 expresses this idea in the words of the wise woman who says to king David after he judges her case, 'my lord the king is *like the Angel of God to discern good and evil*'" (emphasis added).[41]

Discerning good and evil takes us back to the Garden of Eden. As older English translations help us see, Satan's temptation was not to become "like God," but "like gods" (Gen 3:5 KJV, LXX), able to discern good from evil. In fact, Adam and Eve were given the responsibility to discern good from evil at that very moment, as the inspired commentary of Genesis 1-3—that is Psalm 19—explains. It is God's law, however, and not the voice of a fallen heavenly being, that is perfect, that makes wise the simple, that enlightens the eyes (Ps 19:7-9), all language that goes back to the Garden.

Satan, Adam, and Eve all sinned and did the opposite of discerning right and wrong. "Who can discern his errors," (12) the Psalm asks. Only God can keep our sins from having "dominion" (13), more language of the Garden.[42] Thankfully, the Angel of the LORD is the righteous wise judge who never sins. Thus, he is compared to the king, "In order to change

---

[41] David VanDrunen, *Divine Covenants and Moral Order: A Biblical Theology of Natural Law* (Grand Rapids, MI: Eerdmans, 2014), 541.
[42] For a short but fascinating discussion on this see D. J. A. Clines, "The Tree of Knowledge and the Law of Yawheh: Psalm XIX," *VT* 24 (1974), 8-14.

the course of things your servant Joab did this. But my lord has wisdom like the wisdom of the Angel of God to know all things that are on the earth" (2Sa 14:20).

Wisdom and Jesus

In the NT, Jesus tells the Pharisees, "Therefore also the Wisdom of God said, 'I will send them prophets and apostles, some of whom they will kill and persecute'" (Luke 11:49). No one knows if Jesus is referring to some lost text or to the whole OT (much the same way that Hebrews 11:33-38 does) when he brings up Wisdom saying this. But in the parallel account Jesus says, "Therefore *I [Jesus]* send you prophets and wise men and scribes, some of whom you will kill and crucify, and some you will flog in your synagogues and persecute from town to town" (Matt 23:34). Comparing the two, Jesus sees himself as Wisdom, the one who revealed the future to us through prophecy and typology in the OT, the one who created the world.

In the next section, we will look at the strangely related idea of Christ as the Son of God in the OT. The next time you read through Proverbs or any other wisdom book, do more than think of it as wise and practical advice. Think of Christ as being both the Giver and Fulfiller of all that wisdom, for he is the Wisdom of God.

Study Questions:

1. What riches are said to be contained in Christ in Colossians 2:2-3?

2. What attribute more than any other is Solomon known for?

3. How is Wisdom described in Proverbs 8:30, and what was Wisdom doing in this passage?

4. With what do the Jewish Targum say the Lord created the world in Gen 1:1?

5. What is the job of the Angel in 2 Samuel 14:17?

6. What words are interchangeably "sending" in Luke 11:49 and Matthew 23:34?

Part V ‡ Christ Present

The Son of God

The Only-Begotten Son

IN THE NT, A PHRASE occurs identifying Jesus Christ as the "only begotten Son" of God (John 1:14, 18; 3:16; 1Jn 4:9). It is familiar enough, but its origins might not be. This exact Greek phrase does not appear in the OT LXX, so where might it come from? Let's look at two Psalms (Ps 2, 82) and Genesis 1 along with some NT reflections (John 10; Col 1) on these passages for an answer.

The most obvious place where we see something conceptually similar may be Psalm 2:6-7. "I have set my King on Zion, my holy hill. I will tell of the decree: The LORD said to me, 'You are my Son; today I have begotten you.'" This passage is cited several times by the NT as referring to Jesus (Acts 13:33; Heb 1:5; 5:5).

There is a fascinating and deliberate connection between this Psalm and Psalm 82. Consider these two verses: "Ask of me, and I will make the nations your

heritage, and the ends of the earth your possession"
(Ps 2:8). "Arise, O God, judge the earth; for you shall
inherit all the nations!" (Ps 82:8). Psalm 2 has the Son
inheriting the nations, while Psalm 82 has "God" inheriting them. The conceptual parallels between the
two Psalms would suggest that the Son from the one
is God from the other. This is actually what Psalm 82
means, as further reflection demonstrates.

Psalm 82:1 has "God" taking his place in something called "the divine council" (ESV), where "in the
midst of the gods he holds judgment."[43] These "gods"
are called "sons of God" in vs. 6, and when they judge
badly, the foundations of the whole earth shake (vs.
5). The "sons of God" (*beney ha-elohom*) are the heavenly beings that were praising God while he was cre-
ating the universe (Job 38:7). In both the Bible and
neighboring nations, they were considered God's
heavenly royal family.[44]

---

[43] I realize there is controversy among Evangelicals surrounding the
identification of these "gods." For definitive reasons why they cannot
refer to humans see Cyrus Gordon, "אלהים (Elohim) in Its Reputed
Meaning of Rulers, Judges," *Journal of Biblical Literature* 54 (1935):
139–144; W. S. Prinsloo, "Psalm 82: Once Again, Gods or Men?" *Biblica* 76:2 (1995): 219–228; Lowell Handy, "Sounds, Words and Mean-
ings in Psalm 82," *Journal for the Study of the Old Testament* 47 (1990),
51–66; Michael S. Heiser, "Deuteronomy 32:8 and the Sons of God,"
Bibliotheca Sacra 158:629 (Jan-Mar, 2001): 60-72 [52-74].

[44] I have written about this in the Introduction to my book *Giants: Sons
of the Gods*. There is a host of other literature that delves into this as
well. A good place to be introduced to this whole fascinating subject is
the Divine Council website of Dr. Michael Heiser who did his dissertation on the subject. http://www.thedivinecouncil.com/.

Jesus cites Psalm 82:6 to the Pharisees (John 10:34-35). For a host of reasons[45] (not the least of which is the connection between Ps 2 and 82), the best interpretation of this passage is to see Jesus as claiming to be one of these heavenly beings. After all, he has "come down from heaven" (seven times in John 6). When he gives them this passage, it hardly alleviates their anger at his blasphemy, either. This is why they still want to kill him after he quotes the verse. Yet, John 10 makes it clear that Jesus is also different from the other sons of God, for he has a unique relationship to the Father. He is "in" the Father and the Father is "in" him (John 10:38). No other being can say this. Psalm 2 is the same idea, except it uses the term "begotten."

The NT comes along and uses the word "only-begotten" (*monogenes*) and applies it to Jesus. This word means "unique" or "one of a kind," as is easily seen by the fact that Isaac is the "only begotten" son of Abraham (Heb 11:17), even though Abraham had Ishmael 13 years earlier (I think it is actually a double entendra, as it can also mean in some sense, "begotten").[46] Thus, anytime we see "sons of God" or even

---

[45] See Michael S. Heiser, "You've Seen One Elohim, You've Seen Them All? A Critique of Mormonism's Use of Psalm 82," *FARMS Review* 19/1 (2007): 221–266.

[46] On "begotten" see Lee Irons, "The Eternal Generation of the Son," the Upper Register, http://www.upper-register.com/papers/monogenes.html, last accessed 11-4-2019. Basically, two etymologies have been proposed for *monogenes*. "Gennao" (Ps 2:7 LXX) means "to bear, beget." "Genos" means "unique, class, kind." There may even be a

"gods" in the OT, our thought should go to the unique Son of God, the one who created any others who "may be called gods" (1Co 8:5).

Firstborn

Speaking of this creation, in Colossians 1:15-18, the Apostle Paul, reflecting upon creation and Genesis 1, explains, "He is the image of the invisible God, the firstborn of all creation" (15). "God" seems to refer to the Father here. The word "firstborn" is the word *prototokos*. It comes up again in vs. 18 where it says, "And he is the head of the body, the church. He is the beginning, the firstborn (*prototokos*) from the dead, that in everything he might be preeminent." But Paul has not given up his treatment of creation in between these two verses, much less is he saying that this firstborn was created. For he says, "For by him [the firstborn] all things were created, in heaven and on earth, visible and invisible, whether thrones or dominions or rulers or authorities—all things were created through him and for him. And he is before all things, and in him all things hold together" (16-17). Notice how predominate the creation of heavenly beings is in this text.

---

triple entendre going on with this word, as it has very close affinities with "beloved" (as in God's beloved son; Matt 3:17; 17:5; Mark 1:11; 9:7; Luke 3:22; 20:13). "Monogenes," Gerhard Kittel, Geoffrey W. Bromiley, and Gerhard Friedrich, eds., *Theological Dictionary of the New Testament* (Grand Rapids, MI: Eerdmans, 1964–), 739.

But who is this "he," this "firstborn," this "beginning?" Proverbs 8 called him "Wisdom," and this is the connection to our previous chapter. But here, he is deliberately called "His beloved Son" (13). What is amazing about this is how the Church Fathers knew of translations of Genesis 1:1 that went this way: "In the beginning, God became a Son" or "In the beginning, God made for himself a Son."[47] Depending on the exact Greek terms, these may or may not be heretical ideas. However, the Latin Father Jerome states the opinion of people saying, "Most people think that in the Hebrew is contained 'In the Son, God made heaven and earth.'"[48] So whereas the Targum said God created the earth through his Word in Wisdom, this idea has God doing it through the Firstborn Son. This is perfectly orthodox, but how could anyone possibly get this from Genesis 1:1?

The word *reshith* can mean either "beginning" (as most people understand it, i.e. "in the beginning...") or "first," or even the idea of a "firstborn" in Hebrew (cf. Gen 49:3). Thus, the Bible in Basic English reads, "At the first God made the heaven and the earth" (Gen 1:1). In English, "first" can have the idea of either time or rank (the same is true in Greek and Hebrew). If I say, "She was the first in class," I could mean either

---

[47] See Tertullian, *Against Praxeas* 5.1.
[48] Jerome, *Questions in Hebrew, in Genesis i. 507. Quoted in Saint Jerome's Hebrew Questions on Genesis*, trans. C.T. R. Hayward (Oxford: Oxford University Pres, 195), 30.

that she was the first to arrive to the classroom (time), or that she was had the best grades in his class (rank; in my experience, girls were usually first in rank or grades). Paul may in fact have this idea in mind and may be capitalizing on it in Colossians, though as John 1:1's "in the beginning" shows, this would clearly be seen as a flexible idea. So, it is strangely possible to translate Genesis 1:1 with the Firstborn in mind, even as we have seen that it also includes ideas of the Word and Wisdom as well. All of this relates to Christ as the Son of God. The NT is not making up the idea that Christ is the only begotten Son of God. It is getting it from the OT.

At one point, the Gospels tell us that the Son of Man is coming in his glory (Matt 25:31). This is an idea closely associated with Son and other terms we have already discussed. Thus, in the next chapter we will look at Christ: The Glory of God.

Study Questions:

1. What famous adjective(s) is used of God's Son in John 3:16?

2. What does Psalm 2:7 say about the Son?

3. What two figures inherit the nations in Psalm 2:8 and 82:8?

4. Who are the "sons of God" in Job 38:7 and Psalm 82:1, 6?

5. What is Jesus claiming by quoting Psalm 82:6 in John 10:34 that makes the Pharisees still want to kill Jesus for blasphemy?

6. What does *monogenes* ("begotten") mean in Heb 11:17?

7. What word found in Col 1:18 can be substituted for "beginning" in Genesis 1:1?

8. Are "Son" and "Firstborn" interchangeable in Colossians 1:13-18?

Part V ‡ Christ Present

The Glory of God

Heavy Glory

MOST PEOPLE PROBABLY THINK of the glory (Heb. *kabod*; Gk. *doxa*) of God in a very abstract sense, like God's reputation or his honor. "Glory" literally means "to be weighty, full of good things." Certainly "praise" is not far removed from glory either. Each of these are good and right to ascribe to the glory of God. But this is, again, a book on Christ in the OT, and we are going to take a look at how the glory of God is especially related to him.

A good place to start is with Moses. At one point he asks, "Please show me your glory" (Ex 33:18). The glory of the LORD appears in only a couple of places prior to this. In Exodus 16:10, "The glory of the LORD appeared in the cloud." The glory is not the cloud, but it is *in* the cloud. It is difficult to see how or why this would be talking about God's honor or praise due him. We see the same thing eight chapters later when, "The glory of the LORD rested on Mount Sinai, and the cloud covered it for six days; and on the seventh day He called to Moses from the midst of the cloud" (24:16). "He?" I believe the "he" here refers to the Glory, for again, the glory and cloud are separate, and he is calling from inside the cloud.

Before discovering what Moses is actually asking for (and what God gives him in response), consider a couple more things from earlier in Exodus. First, as we saw earlier, Moses has been talking to the Angel of the LORD. This angel had been shrouded in flame (Ex 3:2). But he was also shrouded in cloud. "The angel of God ... moved and went behind them, and the pillar of cloud moved from before them and stood behind them" (Ex 14:19). Just before this, it says that "the LORD" went before them "in a pillar of cloud ... and by night in a pillar of fire" (13:21). Just like the glory, the LORD is in the cloud. On Mount Sinai, "The LORD" promised, "Behold, I am coming to you in a thick cloud" (Ex 19:9). As we have seen, "The glory of the LORD dwelt on Mount Sinai, and the cloud covered it..." (24:16).

The word "dwelt" here is important. It is the verb *shakan*. It is from this that the famous "Shekinah" derives. Shekinah is not a biblical word, but it is found throughout the Aramaic Targums as another buffer word (like Memra/word or Name).[49] Thus, "Jacob awoke from his sleep and said, 'Surely the LORD is in this place, and I did not know it'" (Gen 28:16) becomes, "The Glory of the Lord's Shekinah dwells in this place, and I knew it not (Gen 28:16). "Moses hid his face, for he was afraid to look at God" (Ex 3:6) becomes, "He was afraid to look upon the height of the glory of the Shekinah of the Lord" (Ex 3:6). This last one is interesting for us, because we have seen that it is the Angel of the LORD Moses is afraid to look at.

Now, in Exodus 33, it tells us that Moses entered into the tent and the pillar of cloud would descend and stand at the entrance, and the LORD would speak to Moses (33:9). "The LORD descended in the cloud and stood with him there and proclaimed the Name of the LORD" (34:5). (Recall our discussion of the Name). I'll point out two things here. First, Numbers 12:8 tells us, "With him I speak mouth to mouth, clearly, and not in riddles, and he beholds the form [Heb: *temunah*] of the LORD." The form of the LORD? The Greek translates "form" here as *doxa* or "glory."

Second, there would later be a place where the LORD will choose "to make his Name dwell" (Dt 16:2). And yet, the Psalm says, "O LORD, I love the

---

[49] One Bible dictionary says, "In the later rabbinic sources does the Shekinah become a separate entity created by God as an intermediary between God and man." The same dictionary says, "In the Targums 'shekinah,' 'glory of God,' and 'word of God' are used synonymously. "Glory," in Walter A. Elwell and Barry J. Beitzel, *Baker Encyclopedia of the Bible* (Grand Rapids, MI: Baker Book House, 1988), 1943.

habitation of your house and the place where your glory dwells" (Ps 26:8). We see this emerge clearly in the dedication of the temple by Solomon. First, they bring the ark (God's throne-seat) to the Most Holy Place inside the newly built temple (1Kg 8:6). Then, the "cloud" fills the house of the LORD (10). The LORD now lives here in a special sense, even though the highest heavens cannot contain him. Then, the cloud and glory are linked as God's presence (11). Solomon recognizes that God will dwell in his temple, though the universe cannot contain him (27). Finally, the LORD appears to Solomon (9:1), telling him that now his "Name is there" (3). We are supposed to understand from this that the Name *is the Glory* veiled by the cloud.[50]

The Likeness

One more OT prophet is important to look at here. Ezekiel sees the "likeness as the appearance of a man" (Ezek 1:26). He looked like gleaming metal and his lower body was like fire. He concludes, "This was

---

[50] Meredith Kline believes that the Shekinah-glory is the Holy Spirit ("Kingdom Prologue, Lecture 14," 2012, p. 2; https://faculty.gordon.edu/hu/bi/ted_hildebrandt/digitalcourses/kline_kingdomprologue/kline_kingdom_prologue_text/kline_kingdomprologue_lecture14.pdf, last accessed 11-4-2019). He is close. It is better to see the cloud and fire as images of the Spirit who then enshrouds the Word-Angel-Glory-Name person inside. This is the way the Revelator saw it, "Then I saw another mighty angel coming down from heaven, wrapped in a cloud" (Rev 10:1).

the appearance of the likeness of the Glory of the LORD" (28). Later in the book, the Glory is the LORD (Ezek 9:3-4).

The NT says some pretty amazing things about all this. "And the Word became flesh and dwelt among us, and we have seen his glory, glory as of the only Son from the Father, full of grace and truth" (John 1:14). John equates the *Logos*, the Glory, and the Son. They are all the same thing. It is into this Glory as a Person idea that John later writes, "Isaiah saw his Glory" (Isa 12:41).[51] Read epexegetically[52], Acts 7:55 may very well say, "He [Stephen] … saw the Glory of God, that is Jesus standing at the right hand of God."

And then there is Philippians 2:6-11. Christ exists "in the form of God" and the "likeness of men" (6-7). Recall that Moses beheld the "form [Heb: *temunah*; GK: *doxa*] of the LORD." The Hebrew word was translated as "glory" by the LXX, but that same Hebrew word is translated as "likeness" (*homoioma*) in the Second Commandment (Ex 20:4). This happens to be the word used for "likeness" in Php 2:7. The old hymn here is not saying that Christ only appeared to be one of us but really wasn't. Rather, it is saying that he is the Glory of God. Thus, one dictionary notes,

---

[51] Isaiah 6:1, "I saw the Lord (*Adonai*)" becomes "I saw the Glory of the LORD" (6:1 Isaiah Targum), which becomes, "My eyes have seen the Glory of the Shekinah of the King of the worlds, the Lord of hosts" (Isa 6:5), in the Targum.
[52] Epexegetical refers to adding words to clarify the meaning.

"'Taking the form of a slave', 'becoming in the likeness of men'; and 'being found in the fashion as a man' (vv 7-8) … Phil 2:6 would seem to say that Christ is the divine Glory. The same idea is expressed by the title, 'image of the invisible God"; in the beginning of the hymn of Christ in Col 1:15-20).[53]

In light of all this, it seems to me that Moses was not asking to see the Father (whom Jesus says no man has seen, or can see). He was asking to see the face of the preincarnate Second Person, in whom he was trusting (Heb 11:26); unshrouded from the cloud and fire. God granted that he might see his unshrouded backside, but not his face. Think about this. Moses asks to see God's glory, and he shows him his "backside." This is not an abstract idea or an anthropomorphism but a person. The Glory and the Person are mysteriously united together.

In some ways, it is very similar to the transfiguration of Christ on the mountain where, curiously, Moses also appeared. Peter says, "When he received honor and glory from God the Father, and the voice was borne to him by the Majestic Glory, 'This is my beloved Son, with whom I am well pleased,' we ourselves heard this very voice borne from heaven, for we were

---

[53] J. E. Fossum, "Glory," ed. Karel van der Toorn, Bob Becking, and Pieter W. van der Horst, *Dictionary of Deities and Demons in the Bible* (Leiden; Boston; Köln; Grand Rapids, MI; Cambridge: Brill; Eerdmans, 1999), 351 [348-52]. This entire entry is extremely helpful in grounding our discussion.

with him on the holy mountain" (2Pe 1:17-18). The Glory of the Second Person is omnipresent, but that same Glory is now fully contained in the Person of Jesus Christ. He is the new equivalent of the OT Glory.

In the incarnation, God who said, "'Let light shine out of darkness,' has shone in our hearts to give the light of the knowledge of the glory of God in the face of Jesus Christ" (2Co 4:6). "Arise, shine, for your light has come, and the glory of the LORD has risen upon you" (Isa 60:1). "Therefore it says, 'Awake, O sleeper, and arise from the dead, and Christ will shine on you'" (Eph 5:14).

I said something important a moment ago. Moses asked to see the Glory. God showed him his "face." This is yet another term that becomes equated with the Second Person in the OT, so we will now turn our attention to it.

Study Questions:

1. What does "glory" mean?

2. In Exodus 16:10, where was the glory located?

3. What pronoun is used of "glory" in Exodus 24:16?

4. What Aramaic word is synonymous with "glory?"

5. What does Moses behold in Num 12:8 and what Greek word is used in the LXX for it?

6. What words are interchangeable to describe the "appearance" the prophet saw in Ezekiel 1:26 and 28?

7. What did they behold in John 1:14?

8. What person was Moses asking to see when he asked to see God's glory?

Part V ✠ Christ Present

The Face of God

A Representing Face

"FACE" IS A TERM that we use even today both literally and symbolically. Obviously, all people have faces. But if I asked you who was the "face" of the Denver Broncos, if you knew anything at all about the organization, you would have to say John Elway. In this case, "face" is being used symbolically for the representative figurehead of the organization. Can we speak of God in this way?

The first use of "face" in this way is probably not even recognizable, making for a kind of irony, since that's the whole point of representative faces. Genesis 3:8 says, "The man and his wife hid themselves from the presence of the LORD God among the trees of the garden." The word "presence" is the word *paneh*. It is very often translated as "face." For example, when Hagar flees from Sarah, she flees from her "face" (Gen

16:6 LXX; KJV). To flee from the presence of face is to flee from a *person*, not a mere thing.

Several Church Fathers believed that Adam was hiding from Christ. For example, "The God and Father, indeed, cannot be contained, and is not found in a place, for there is no place of His rest; but His Word, through whom He made all things, being His Power and His Wisdom, assuming the role of the Father and Lord of all, went to the garden and conversed with Adam" (Theophilus of Antioch, *To Autolycus* 2.22).

The Face-Form

In Numbers 12:6-8, God says,

> Hear my words: If there is a prophet among you, I the LORD make myself known to him in a vision; I speak with him in a dream. Not so with my servant Moses. He is faithful in all my house. With him I speak mouth to mouth, clearly, and not in riddles, and he beholds the form of the LORD.

This has a parallel in Exodus 33:11, "Thus the LORD used to speak to Moses face to face, as a man speaks to his friend."

If Moses saw a form, what did it look like? We do not have an exact answer to that. In fact, we have two distinct trajectories that keep us from speculating too much. On one hand, Moses has this famous and yet confusing encounter with the LORD on Mt. Sinai.

Immediately after telling us that Moses speaks to God "face to face," we learn that the "Presence" of God will go with Israel in the wilderness (Ex 33:14). "Face" and "Presence" are the same word we saw in Genesis 3:8. Moses is immediately glad and says, "If your presence does not go with us, do not lead us up from here." They need the LORD!

But then, the discussion takes a turn. Moses says, "Show me your Glory" (18). God's response is curious. "'I will make all my goodness pass before you and will proclaim before you my Name 'The LORD.' And I will be gracious to whom I will be gracious and will show mercy on whom I will show mercy. But,' he said, 'You cannot see my face, for man shall not see me and live'" (19). Moses asks to see God's Glory; God says you cannot see my Face. This seems to equate the Face with the Glory.

Nevertheless, God's Glory does pass by, but it is shielded somehow by God's Hand (22; which we will look at in the next section). This "shielding" effect, what the passage here calls God's "backside" (23), is similar in nature that the other fact, which is that Moses has in fact seen God many times, albeit shrouded by fire or a cloud or incense. The points us right back the Angel. It seems that what Moses wanted was to see God "in the nude" as Martin Luther might put it. But the LORD satisfied Moses' curiosity by simply giving him more of Christ. This was in Christ proclaimed and in Christ shrouded. Again, this makes me think of the Transfiguration, where the veiled human Christ was somehow unveiled into a glorious being of light, and Moses was there bearing witness. Nevertheless, the Apostles did not glimpse the Father, but still only the Son, albeit in resplendent glory.

The Angel-Face

At this point, it is helpful to return to the Angel of the LORD. That important passage in Exodus 23:20-22 must be looked at now in light of the face. The text literally says, "Behold, I send an angel before you to guard you on the way and to bring you to the place that I have prepared. Pay careful attention to his face/presence and obey his voice; do not rebel against him, for he will not pardon your transgression, for my name is in him" (20:20-21). While many translations leave "face" completely untranslated, it is a very important aspect of the Angel.

This is made clear by Isaiah where, in a very important passage he says, "In all their affliction he was afflicted, and the Angel of his Presence/Face saved them; in his love and in his pity he redeemed them; he lifted them up and carried them all the days of old" (Isa 63:9). Thus, he is literally given the title: The Angel of the Presence or The Angel of the Face. In this way, he is God's representative to his people in the OT.

The NT picks up on this language as well. The Apostle says, "For God, who said, 'Let light shine out of darkness,' has shone in our hearts to give the light of the knowledge of the Glory of God in the Face of Jesus Christ" (2Co 4:6). The Apostle is alluding here to Genesis 1:3, which is God's Word speaking light into existence, and to Isaiah 9:2 which is a deeply Christological text, as we see from Matthews quotation of it in Matt 4:15-16.

And then there are passages like the following on in John's Gospel. Notice the confluence of terms that we have discussed coming together here.

> The Father who sent me has himself borne witness about me. His voice you have never heard, his *form* you have never seen, and you do not have his word abiding in you, for you do not believe the one whom he has sent. You search the Scriptures because you think that in them you have eternal life; and it is they that bear witness about me, but you refuse to come to me that you may have life … I have come in my Father's *name*, and you do not receive me. If another comes in his own *name*, you will receive him. How can you believe, when you receive *glory* from one another and do not seek the *glory* that comes from the only God? Do not think that I will accuse you to the Father. There is one who accuses you: Moses, on whom you have set

your hope. For if you believed Moses, you would believe me; for he wrote of me. But if you do not believe his writings, how will you believe my words?"

(John 5:37-40, 43-47)

Study Questions:

1. What Hebrew word is translated as both "face" and "presence?"

2. When Moses asked to see God's Glory, what did God say he could not see?

3. What does Isaiah call the Angel in Isaiah 63:9.

4. What is an important NT passage that talks about Christ as the Face of God?

Part V ✠ Christ Present

The Right-Hand of God

God's Arm and Right Hand

"WHO HAS BELIEVED what he has heard from us? And to whom has the arm of the LORD been revealed?" asks the prophet (Isa 53:1), as he begins his lengthy and mysterious prophecy of the Suffering Servant, which is probably the high-water mark for all Messianic prophecies in the OT. The Arm or Right Hand of the LORD is, like several of the terms we have looked at, easy to misunderstand.

When people think of the "arm" of the LORD, many probably anthropomorphize the idea. God doesn't literally have an arm, any more than he literally has eyes or wings. God is Spirit. Of course, I wholeheartedly agree with this, in as much as I am talking about the One Being called God. However, when the Bible speaks of God's Arm or his Right Hand (see Dt 4:34; 9:29; 26:8), it has something more concrete in mind than merely symbolizing God vis-à-vis personification.

The "Right Hand" in the ancient world was a way of describing a position or seat of great authority and power that a particular individual, such as a general or captain, holds under the command of the king. We saw previously how Christ, the Commander of the LORD's army (Josh 5:14; cf. Ex 15:3), identified himself as the Angel of the LORD to Joshua saying, "Take off your sandals from your feet, for the place where you are standing is holy" (Josh 5:15, cf. Ex 3:5). In the NT, God seated Christ "at his right hand in the heavenly places, far above all rule and authority and power and dominion, and above every name that is named" (Eph 1:20-21), after he "disarmed" and "triumphed over them" (Col 2:15), having made them subject to him (1Pe 3:22). This refers to Jesus' victory as King of kings and Lord of lords.

The Arm of the LORD is a way of talking about this Commander or this Right Hand. We can see that the Arm and Right Hand of God are related in the same way a human hand and arm are related by not identical. "You have a mighty Arm; strong is your Hand, high your Right Hand" (Ps 89:13). The Arm seems to be what the Right hand (man) carries out. The Arm stands for military power (Dt 4:34; Isa

30:30), creative power (Isa 51:9; Ps 89:11, 14),[54] and God as a judge (Isa 51:5).

Let's take a more detailed look now at the Arm as it is described in the Exodus, especially as it regards salvation and judgment. The first verse describing it says, "I will redeem you with an outstretched Arm" (Ex 6:6). We find this salvation theme with the Right Hand and/or Arm in other places as well (Ps 98:1; Isa 33:2; 52:10). Moses then sings of the beginning of this prophetic fulfillment, "Terror and dread fall upon them; because of the greatness of your Arm, they are still as a stone, till your people, O LORD, pass by, till the people pass by whom you have purchased" (Ex 15:16). Who shall do this? "The LORD is a man of war; the LORD is his Name" (15:3). (Notice again the "Name" theme). Moses sees the Arm of the LORD as the man of war, Yahweh, the angel of Yahweh, who is later called the LORD of Hosts or Armies (Hos 12:4-5).

Isaiah reflects on this very same thing and says, "Where is he who brought them up out of the sea with the shepherds of his flock? Where is he who put in the midst of them his Holy Spirit, who caused his

---

[54] These texts combine the original creation and God's mythical battle with the sea monster from pagan stories with the new creation God is doing in his military battle at the Exodus as he assaults and defeats Rahab, the Egyptian-Pharaonic "sea monster." For more on the connection to the Exodus, Pharaoh, and how the arm is "the vehicle by which he conquers see J. K. Hoffmeier, "The Arm of God versus the Arm of Pharaoh in the Exodus Narratives," Bib 67 (1986): 378–87; last accessed 8-29-2014.

glorious Arm to go at the right hand of Moses, who divided the waters before them to make for himself an everlasting name" (Isa 63:11-12). This time we can see the relationship between the Arm and the Name. But dictionaries are very provocative when they boldly assert things like, "'Arm' is used as a hypostasis in Isa 63:12. Here the *zeroa* stands for an independent power going side by side with Moses and stressing the function of Yhwh as Shepherd and leader of his people."[55] "Hypostasis" is exactly how Christians describe the divine and human natures in the One Person of Jesus Christ (the hypostatic union) and the relationship between the Father, Son, and Holy Spirit (Three *Hypostases*) to the Godhead (in one *Ousia*). We've seen this idea now with the Word, the Name, and the Glory.

Jesus as Arm

Into this theology, the last chapter of the Bible has Jesus himself saying, "Behold, I am coming soon, bringing my recompense with me, to repay each one for what he has done" (Rev 22:12). This is a paraphrase of Isaiah 40:10 and the Messianic prophecy that says, "Behold, the Lord GOD (*Adonai Yahweh*) comes with might, and his Arm rules for him; behold, his reward is with him, and his recompense before

---

[55] B. Becking, "Arm," ed. Karel van der Toorn and Pieter W. van der Horst, *Dictionary of Deities and Demons in the Bible* (Leiden; Boston; Köln; Grand Rapids, MI; Cambridge: Brill; Eerdmans, 1999), 90.

him." Thus, Greg Beale concludes, "What is prophesied of the Lord in Isaiah is now prophesied by Jesus to be fulfilled by himself."[56] No wonder then that Jude says Jesus saved a people out of the land of Egypt (Jude 1:5, see Part II).

Thus, in answer to the original question of this chapter, John's Gospel says, "Though he had done so many signs before them, they still did not believe in him, so that the word spoken by the prophet Isaiah might be fulfilled: "Lord, who has believed what he heard from us, and to whom has the Arm of the Lord been revealed?" (John 12:37-38). Indeed, Jesus is the Arm the LORD, the great military commander who carries out justice on the earth, and who powerfully saves his people.

But the people were wrong in their view of him. They thought he would be a military commander who would crush the head of the Roman beast. Instead, Isaiah predicted this salvation would come through a great twist of irony. The Arm of the LORD would be revealed through the Suffering Servant. He would win the victory alright, but it would be a victory over sin, death, and the devil by suffering and dying for our sins and being raised from the dead. Truly, his Right Arm is Glorious.

---

[56] G. K. Beale and D. A. Carson, *Commentary on the New Testament Use of the Old Testament* (Grand Rapids, MI; Nottingham, UK: Baker Academic; Apollos, 2007), 1156.

Study Questions:

1. In the ancient world, what does the "right hand" describe?

2. How is the Angel described in Joshua 5:14 and Exodus 15:3?

3. Where is Christ seated at his ascension (Eph 1:20-21; 1 Pet 3:22)?

4. In Psalm 89:13, what does the mighty hand stand for?

5. How does God redeem in Exodus 6:6?

6. What term that we use to describe the union between Christ's human and divine natures did we say is also used to describe the glorious arm in Isaiah 63:11-12?

7. Revelation 22:12 borrows from Isaiah 40:10 and replaces "his arm" with what person?

Part V ✠ Christ Present

The Good Shepherd

A Metaphor?

Life has changed drastically in the western world during the past couple of centuries. For example, whereas at the founding of the United States, the vast majority of people owned land and were farmers, today it is the reverse. Many own no real land to speak of, nor do they make their living off it. Our agrarian culture of green pastures has become a civilization of city lights and cold cement. This has taken us at least in some ways out of touch with metaphors the Bible uses to describe God.

One such metaphor is "shepherd." Jesus famously told the people, "I am the Good Shepherd" (John 10:11, 14). This is picked up later by his disciples. Peter calls Jesus, "the Shepherd and Overseer of your souls" (1Pe 2:25) and "the Chief Shepherd" (5:4). Hebrews calls him "the Great Shepherd of the sheep" (Heb 13:20). But why did Jesus use this language of himself? Was he simply trying to capture a metaphor that the people of those days could relate to? My guess is that this may be the default view of many Christians.

In fact, the language is taken from prophecies regarding the Messiah. The most explicit is probably Zechariah 13:7. "'Awake, O sword, against my Shepherd, against the man who stands next to me,' declares the LORD of hosts. 'Strike the Shepherd, and the sheep will be scattered; I will turn my hand against the little ones.'" The "man who stands next to me" is a war term for the Right Hand. Now we want to note that this man is called a "Shepherd." This is confirmed by the NT, which directly quotes the last part of the verse. "Then Jesus said to them, 'You will all fall away because of me this night. For it is written, 'I will strike the shepherd, and the sheep of the flock will be scattered'" (Matt 26:31; Mark 14:27). Jesus directly applied this prophecy to himself.

There are other prophecies that speak of him as Shepherd. "But you, O Bethlehem Ephrathah, who are too little to be among the clans of Judah, from you shall come forth for me one who is to be ruler in Israel, whose coming forth is from of old, from ancient days … he shall stand and shepherd his flock in the strength of the LORD, in the majesty of the name of the LORD his God. And they shall dwell secure, for now he shall be great to the ends of the earth" (Mic 5:2, 4).

The first part of this passage is also quoted by the NT (Matt 2:6; cf. John 7:2) as referring to Jesus. Since it is the same person in view throughout, Jesus is thus predicted to be the Shepherd here.

Notice how this shepherd stands "in the majesty of the Name of the LORD his God." Earlier, we discussed the Name and saw how it is a term that also hypostatically identifies the Son of God. We've seen the same with "Arm." Thus, it comes as little surprise at this point to see Isaiah predicting, "Behold, the Lord GOD comes with might, and his Arm rules for him; behold, his reward is with him, and his recompense before him. He will tend his flock like a shepherd ..." (Isa 40:10-11). This passage is again cited in the NT as referring to Jesus (Rev 22:12). So, we have established that the title of "Shepherd" comes from prophecies in the OT.

Shepherds, Kings, and Gods

But could there be more to it than the prophets simply taking a metaphor and applying it to the Messiah? Ezekiel predicts, "And I will set up over them one Shepherd, my servant David, and he shall feed them: he shall feed them and be their Shepherd" (Ezek 34:23). Again, this is a Messianic prophecy. Ezekiel is not predicting the reincarnation of David, but a future leader who comes from his line: "The Son of David" (Matt 9:27, etc.).

Now, kings of the ancient world were often called "shepherds." It's a rather ironic title, because shepherd is a lowly profession, filled with long hot days, dangers from animals and cliffs and thickets, mockery from townsfolk, and lots and lots of tedium. Why give such a glorious office as king a title like "shepherd?" The answer is that it gets at the difficult task they were assigned to look over their people, who are often innocent but dumb as sheep.

But what do I mean *assigned*? Many ancient cultures taught in one form or another that kingship was given by the gods. For example, the ancient myth of Etana, a Sumerian antediluvian King of Kish says, "Scepter, crown, tiara, and (shepherd's) crook lay deposited before Anu in heaven | There being no counseling for its people. (Then) kingship descended from heaven." This is exactly what the Bible teaches when we learn that God himself chose Saul to be king, effectively, in his place. That is, Israel had rejected Yahweh as their king, therefore he chooses Saul and later David. They did not take this position of their own accord. God chose them. Kingship came from him, from heaven.

Notice how in the myth, king Etana is called a "shepherd." This is as we find it in the Bible too. God said to David, "You shall be shepherd of my people

Israel, and you shall be prince over Israel" (2Sa 5:2). Curiously, Joshua is the first Israelite leader called a "shepherd" (Num 27:17-18). He, too, is chosen by the LORD. When kings like Jehoshaphat did not lead well, Israel was said to be "as sheep that have no shepherd" (1Kg 22:17). Why is that curious? Because in Greek, his name is "Jesus."

Let's put this idea of kingship coming down from heaven together with this notion that kings are called shepherds. Throughout the ancient world, the gods (or better, the sons of God) are called shepherds too. Baal (KTU 1.12.II), Adonis (Virgil, *Eclogues*), Osiris depicted often with his shepherd's crook staff, Tammuz (Babylon), and others are all called shepherds of the sheep.

Where this gets really curious is in the book of 1 Enoch. 1 Enoch 89:59 describes "seventy shepherds" of the nations. Who are they here? Charles writes, "The 'seventy shepherds' raise the most vexed question in Enoch." Yet, while they may in a more immediate way represent humans, on another level, the level of paralleling heaven and earth, "They are certainly angels [which correspond to the seventy sons of God from Babel]."[57] I agree. With the Jews, seventy

---

[57] Robert Henry Charles, ed., *Commentary on the Pseudepigrapha of the Old Testament*, vol. 2 (Oxford: Clarendon Press, 1913), 255. For discussions see John J. Collins, *The Apocalyptic Imagination: An Introduction to Jewish Apocalyptic Literature* (Eerdmans, 2016), 87-89; and Margaret Barker, *The Revelation of Jesus Christ* (Edinburgh: T&T Clark, 2000), 226-29.

was always used in one way or another with this divine council theology in mind.

Christ is My Shepherd

Let's now take this over to our discussion of Christ in the OT as the Son of God who inherits Israel and then the nations. Returning to an earlier text, there is a reason why Jacob says, "The God before whom my fathers Abraham and Isaac walked, the God who has been my shepherd all my life long to this day, the angel who has redeemed me from all evil, bless the boys" (Gen 48:15-16). This idea fits perfectly with the entire ancient world's conception of the sons of God as shepherds. Israel's God-Son is the Angel.

The Psalm says, "Give ear, O Shepherd of Israel, you who lead Joseph like a flock. You who are enthroned upon the cherubim, shine forth" (Ps 80:1). Who is it who comes to the Most Holy Place? Whose seat is the Mercy Seat? Yahweh, the Son of God (Lev 16:2).

Then, of course, in that most famous of all OT verses, David sings, "The LORD is my Shepherd" (Ps 23:1). What is he singing? He is singing about his Lord (Adonai), the Lord who stands between him and the Father Yahweh, yet as his own Lord, as Jesus taught the Pharisees (Matt 22:44-45). This is why Jesus takes the title of Shepherd upon himself. Every use of the term as it refers to God in prophecy or in history in the OT speaks of him.

Just as the Pharaohs knew Aman-Ra as their shepherd and Assurbanipal knew Shamash as his shepherd (*"Light of the great gods, resplendent illuminator of the universe, Lofty judge, shepherd of the celestial and earthly regions"*),[58] so also David knew the Son of God as his Shepherd. Except, his Shepherd is not just a shepherd, but The Shepherd, the Shepherd who would soon humble himself in the womb of a virgin, be born at Bethlehem Ephrathah, come to shepherd his flock in the strength of the LORD in the majesty of the Name of the LORD his God, where the sheep shall dwell secure, and he shall be great to the ends of the earth. Never view "Shepherd" language in the OT apart from Christ again. For, In calling the LORD his Shepherd, David is effectively saying that Christ is his Shepherd. All this in the Old Testament.

---

[58] COS 1.143:474. In T. Longman III, "Psalms 2: Ancient Near Eastern Background," ed. Peter Enns, *Dictionary of the Old Testament: Wisdom, Poetry & Writings* (Downers Grove, IL; Nottingham, England: IVP Academic; Inter-Varsity Press, 2008), 601.

Study Questions:

1. List several places where Jesus is identified as a Shepherd in the NT.

2. List several places where a Shepherd is prophesied in the OT.

3. Several nations referred to their gods as shepherds. List three of them.

4. When David sings that the LORD is his Shepherd, of whom is he singing? Do you think that this means that David knew this person personally?

Part VI ‡ Conclusion

THROUGHOUT THIS BOOK, we have looked at how Jesus gives us his own key for interpreting the Bible. This key is to see him in all the Scripture. When a person does this, it is the key to life itself, for it opens the way by which we may come to him. We have seen many NT passages that explicitly teach that Jesus was in the OT. We have learned how prophecy, typology, and the law each point to him in their own unique ways. We have also seen how there are certain words and ideas that profoundly and mysteriously describe an actual person in the OT, a person who is present with his people, who walks among them, who fights for them, who delivers them, who covenants with them, but who had not yet come in the flesh. It is patently obvious that they knew him. We have seen ten ideas—that he is the Angel, the Word, the Power, the Name, the Wisdom, The Son, the Glory, the Face, the Arm, and the Shepherd.

None of these ideas are original to me; all have been written about by scholars, in journals, books, Bible dictionaries, etc. to one degree or another. Also, it isn't that in this book I am somehow saying that all prophecy is about Christ *in the same way*, or that there is no such thing as anthropomorphism in this list of words (sure there are, we can think of each of these in the more abstract senses too), etc. But rather that in some ways, Christ is related to all of these things. Not in every way, but in some ways. I am not presenting you with an either/or, but a both/and. I just happen to be talking about Christ at this time.

To conclude this thought, I want to turn to Hebrews. Hebrews speaks of prophets, types, and law all in the context of Jesus fulfilling them. But in an absolutely fascinating opening to this book-sermon, Hebrews does something amazing with all of the individual words we have been looking at. It begins by telling us how Christ is superior to angels. After writing most of these chapters, I was flabbergasted to discover that we find nine of these ten word-ideas being applied to Christ in the span of just five verses. "In these last days [God] has spoken to us by his *Son*" (Heb 1:2). "He is the radiance of the *Glory* of God," the exact *imprint* of his nature (1:3).[59] "He upholds the universe by the *word* of his *power*" (1:3). "He sat down at the *right hand*

---

[59] The "imprint" is an idea closely associated with the image of God, and thus God's Face.

of the Majesty on high" (1:3). "Having become as much superior to *angels* as the *Name* he has inherited is more excellent than theirs" (1:4). "When the brings the *firstborn*[60] into the world, he says, 'Let all God's angels worship him'" (1:6). If we add the first verse of the book, we see the first three categories we talked about (prophecy, typology, law): "Long ago, at many times and in many ways, God spoke to our fathers by the prophets" (Heb 1:1). And if we add one of the last verses of the book, its benediction, we see the Shepherd. "Now may the God of peace who brought again from the dead our Lord Jesus, the great *Shepherd* of the sheep, by the blood of the eternal covenant, equip you with everything good that you may do his will, working in us that which is pleasing in his sight, through Jesus Christ, to whom be glory forever and ever. Amen" (Heb 13:20-21).

Whoever wrote this letter, "got it." Of course he did! He was inspired by God himself. But he also interpreted the Scripture using the basic principle that Jesus taught him. Clearly, the original authors knew and applied each of these ideas to Christ. Their hearts were saturated with seeing him as is was in the OT, and as he became at his incarnation.

I hope that this book has shown you that learning to see Christ in the OT is both a science and an art. It

---

[60] Recall our discussion of "first" and "firstborn" in the chapter on Wisdom and then the chapter on the Son.

takes knowledge, desire, and practice. The more you do it, the better you should get. Nevertheless, it is not always easy to do this correctly, and many have made mistakes. In fact, all of us have.

Some have seen Christ where he probably is not. By not using sound rules of interpretation, by wanting to see things that aren't there, or by not understanding that there is more than one way to see Christ in the OT, they have not interpreted the Scripture as best they could. But others—sadly many others—have failed to see him where he clearly is, often in many, many places where he is to be found in the OT, in places that I believe OT peoples would themselves have had at least an inkling of some kind of plurality in a kind of Godhead.

People often ask me about this. "Then who should try?" Well, we all "try," to one degree or another. Putting into practice this question is unavoidable. The question is, will you follow the Savior's hermeneutic, or one of your own making?

This can be a frightening business, for who wants to misinterpret God's word? I've often told people that on The Day, when I face the LORD in judgment, he may very well ask me how I handled his word. Perhaps he would ask me one of two questions. The first, "Doug, why did you see my Son in places he was not?" The second, "Doug, why did not you see my Son in places where he is to be found?" As for me, I guess I would much rather err by seeing too much of the Savior than not enough, especially given his own explicit teaching on this subject and the reprimand he gave the ordinary (non-Apostolic) disciple Cleopas and his unnamed friend on the road to Emmaus. He expected they would do this. I do not desire to read and teach the Bible as an end to itself. The Pharisees read it in just this way and would not come to Christ to have life (John 5:40).

How about you?

Works Cited

Baker Encyclopedia of the Bible. Ed. Walter A. Elwell and Barry J. Beitzel. Grand Rapids, MI: Baker Book House, 1988.

Barker, Margaret. *The Revelation of Jesus Christ.* Edinburgh: T&T Clark, 2000.

Bauckham, Richard. "The Throne of God and the Worship of Jesus." In *The Jewish Roots of Christological Monotheism: Papers from the St. Andrews Conference on the Historical Origins of the Worship of Jesus.* Ed. C. Newman, J. Davila, and G. Lewis. Leiden: E. J. Brill, 1999.

Becking, B. "Arm." In *Dictionary of Deities and Demons in the Bible.* Ed. Karel van der Toorn and Pieter W. van der Horst. Leiden; Boston; Köln; Grand Rapids, MI; Cambridge: Brill; Eerdmans, 1999.

Bruce, F. F. *The Epistle to the Galatians: a Commentary on the Greek Text,* New International Greek Testament Commentary. Grand Rapids, MI: W.B. Eerdmans Pub. Co., 1982.

Boyarin, Daniel. "The Gospel of the Memra: Jewish Binitarianism and the Prologue to John." *Harvard Theological Review* 94:3 (2001): 243-84.

Calvin, John. *Commentary on Genesis.*

Cathcart, Kevin; Maher, Michael; and McNamara, Martin eds. *The Aramaic BibleA: Targum Neofiti 1: Genesis,* trans. Martin McNamara, vol. 1. Collegeville, MN: The Liturgical Press, 1992.

Charles, Robert H. *Commentary on the Pseudepigrapha of the Old Testament,* vol. 2. Oxford: Clarendon Press, 1913.

Clines, D.J.A. "The Tree of Knowledge and the Law of Yawheh: Psalm XIX." *VT* 24 (1974): 8-14.

Commentary on the New Testament Use of the Old Testament. Ed. G. K. Beale and D. A. Carson. Grand Rapids, MI; Nottingham, UK: Baker Academic; Apollos, 2007.

Collins, John J. *The Apocalyptic Imagination: An Introduction to Jewish Apocalyptic Literature.* Eerdmans, 2016.

Dictionary of the Old Testament: Wisdom, Poetry & Writings. Ed. Peter Enns. Downers Grove, IL; Nottingham, England: IVP Academic; Inter-Varsity Press, 2008.

Edwards, M. J. "Justine's Logos and the Word of God." *JECS* 3 (1995): 261-80.

Fossum, J. E. "Glory." In *Dictionary of Deities and Demons in the Bible.* Ed. Karel van der Toorn, Bob Becking, and Pieter W. van der Horst. Leiden; Boston; Köln; Grand Rapids, MI; Cambridge: Brill; Eerdmans, 1999.

Gordon, Cyrus. "אלהים (Elohim) in Its Reputed Meaning of Rulers, Judges." *Journal of Biblical Literature* 54 (1935): 139–144.

Goulder, Michael. *Midrash and Lection in Matthew: The Speaker's Lectures in Biblical Studies, 1969-71.* London: SPCK, 1974.

Heiser, Michael S. "Deuteronomy 32:8 and the Sons of God," *Bibliotheca Sacra* 158:629 (Jan-Mar, 2001): 52-74.

_____. "Divine Council," in Tremper Longman III and Peter Enns, eds., *Dictionary of the Old Testament: Wisdom, Poetry & Writings.* Downers Grove, IL; Nottingham, England: IVP Academic; Inter-Varsity Press, 2008.

_____. *The Myth That is True.* Unpublished.

_____. *The Unseen Realm.* Bellingham, WA: Lexham, 2015.

_____. "Why Use the Septuagint." LogosTalk (Dec 2007). https://blog.logos.com/2007/12/why_use_the_septuagint/, last accessed 5-4-2015.

. "You've Seen One Elohim, You've Seen Them All? A Critique of Mormonism's Use of Psalm 82." *FARMS Review* 19/1 (2007): 221–266.

Hendriksen, William and Kistemaker, Simon J. *Exposition of the Gospel According to Matthew*, vol. 9. New Testament Commentary. Grand Rapids: Baker Book House, 1953–2001.

Hoffmeier, J. K. "The Arm of God versus the Arm of Pharaoh in the Exodus Narratives." *Bib* 67 (1986): 378–87.

Huffmon, H. B. "Name." In *Dictionary of Deities and Demons in the Bible*. Ed. Karel van der Toorn, Bob Becking, and Pieter W. van der Horst. Leiden; Boston; Köln; Grand Rapids, MI; Cambridge: Brill; Eerdmans, 1999.

Hurtado, Larry. "The Binitarian Shape of Early Christian Worship." *In The Jewish Roots of Christological Monotheism: Papers from the St. Andrews Conference on the Historical Origins of the Worship of Jesus.* Ed. C. Newman, J. Davila, and G. Lewis. Leiden: E. J. Brill, 1999.

Irons, Lee. "The Eternal Generation of the Son." http://www.upper-register.com/papers/monogenes.html. Last accessed 8-15-2014.

Kline, Meredith G. "Kingdom Prologue, Lecture 14." 2012. https://faculty.gordon.edu/hu/bi/ted_hildebrandt/digital-courses/kline_kingdomprologue/kline_kingdom_pro-logue_text/kline_kingdomprologue_lecture14.pdf. Last Accessed 8-16-2014.

Metzger, Bruce Manning. *A Textual Commentary on the Greek New Testament, Second Edition a Companion Volume to the United Bible Societies' Greek New Testament (4th Rev. Ed.).* United Bible Societies. London; New York: United Bible Societies, 1994.

Orlov, Andrei A. *The Etymology of the Name 'Metatron," in The Enoch-Metatron Tradition.* TSAJ, 107; Tuebiingen: Mohr-Sieback, 2005.

Pao David W., and Schnabel, Eckhard J. "Luke." In *Commentary on the New Testament Use of the Old Testament*. Ed. G. K. Beale and D. A. Carson. Grand Rapids, MI; Nottingham, UK: Baker Academic; Apollos, 2007.

Prinsloo, W. S. "Psalm 82: Once Again, Gods or Men?" *Biblica* 76:2 (1995): 219–228.

Segal, Alan F. *Two Powers in Heaven: Early Rabbinic Reports about Christianity and Gnosticism.* SJLA 25. Leiden: E. J. Brill, 1977.

Theological Dictionary of the New Testament. Kittel, Gerhard; Bromiley, Geoffrey W.; and Friedrich, Gerhard eds. Grand Rapids, MI: Eerdmans, 1964– .

Van Dorn, Douglas. *Giants: Sons of the Gods.* Erie, CO: Waters of Creation Publishing, 2013.

_____. *Waters of Creation: A Biblical-Theological Study of Baptism.* Erie, Co: Waters of Creation Pub., 2009.

VanDrunen, David. *Divine Covenants and Moral Order: A Biblical Theology of Natural Law.* Grand Rapids, MI: Eerdmans, 2014.

Vos, Geerhardus. *Biblical Theology.* Grand Rapids, MI: Eerdmans, 1948.

Welty, Greg. "Eschatological Fulfillment and the Confirmation of Mosaic Law." http://www.the-highway.com/mosaic-law_Welty.html. Last accessed, 8-14-2014.

Also cited:

Church Fathers: Justin Martyr, Pseudo-Ignatius, Irenaeus, Tertullian, Cyprian, Novatian, Eusebius, Athanasius, Hilary of Poitiers, Gregory Nazianzen, Basil, Ambrose, Chrysostom, Augustine, Jerome, Cyril, Socrates Scholasticus, Constitutions of the Holy Apostles.

Jewish: Philo, Josephus, Genesis Rabbah, the Targums, and the Babylonian Talmud.

All pictures are found in the public domain.

Author Index

Scripture Index

ABOUT THE AUTHOR

Doug has pastored the Reformed Baptist Church of Northern Colorado since 2001. He graduated from Bethel College in 1992, majoring in Marketing and minoring in Bible. He was a youth pastor for four years in Denver. He holds the Master of Divinity degree from Denver Seminary (2001).

Doug has served on councils and boards for two Baptist Associations, the current one which he helped found in 2016. The Reformed Baptist Network seeks to glorify God through fellowship and cooperation in fulfilling the Great Commission to the ends of the earth. There are currently 42 churches in this international association of churches.

Doug has co-hosted the radio show Journey's End, the Peeranormal podcast, started the Waters of Creation Publishing Company, owned two small business in Minneapolis, and has appeared on numerous podcasts and radio shows.

Married since 1994, he and Janelle are the proud parents of four beautiful young girls. Born and raised in Colorado, he has climbed all 54 of Colorado's 14,000 ft. mountains and also Mt. Rainier (WA) and Mt. Shasta (CA).

To find out more about any of these things go to:
https://www.dougvandorn.com/

The Church website is
https://rbcnc.com

Books in the Christ In All Scripture Series

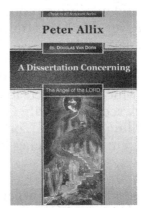

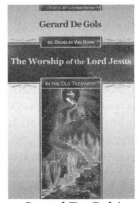

John Owen's treatment is perfect for those wanting to ground their theology of the Angel in the high orthodoxy of the Reformation. The quotations from the Fathers bolster his thesis.

Peter Allix's work is comprehensive and is especially helpful for those familiar with modern scholarship wishing to root their theology in conservative Protestant/Reformed orthodoxy.

Gerard De Gols' study, especially the second half, is imminently practical and would help anyone wanting to learn more about why it matters that Christ is present in the Old Testament.

Owen, Allix, and De Gols together in one volume, minus quotations from the Fathers and Reformers.

The Second Edition of *From the Shadows to the Savior*, it explores even more of the titles given to Christ in the OT than Allix goes into.

Practical sermons are for the further exploration of the fullness of Christ, especially as he is found in the NT.

Other Books by Doug Van Dorn

Giants: Sons of the Gods

The bestselling non-fiction book on Genesis 6 and the Nephilim.
150 reviews. 4.5+++ stars on Amazon.

Goliath. You know the story. But why is it in the Bible? Is it just to give us a little moral pick-me-up as we seek to emulate a small shepherd boy who defeated a giant? Have you ever wondered where Goliath came from? Did you know he had brothers, one with 24 fingers and toes? Did you know their ancestry is steeped in unimaginable horror? Genesis 6. The Nephilim. The first few verses of this chapter have long been the speculation of supernatural events that produced demigods and a flood that God used to destroy the whole world. The whole world remembers them. Once upon a time, all Christians knew them. But for many centuries this view was mocked, though it was the only known view at the time of the writing of the New Testament. Today, it is making a resurgence among Bible-believing scholars, and for good reason. The Nephilim were on the earth in those days, and also afterward...

This book delves deep into the dark and ancient recesses of our past to bring you rich treasures long buried. It is a carefully researched, heavily footnoted, and selectively illustrated story of the giants of the Bible. There is more here than meets the eye, much more. Here you will learn the invisible, supernatural storyline of the Bible that is always just beneath the surface, lurking like the spawn of the ancient leviathan. It is a storyline no person can afford to ignore any longer. Unlike other more sensational books on the topic, there is no undue speculation to be found here. The author is a Bible-believing Christian who refuses to use such ideas to tell you the end of the world is drawing nigh. Once you discover the truth about these fantastic creatures, you will come to see the ministry and work of Jesus Christ in a very new and exalting light. Come. Learn the fascinating, sobering, yet true story of real giants who played a significant role in the bible ... and still do so today.

Available in Paperback or Kindle at Amazon.com

Q & A COMPANION

THE
UNSEEN
REALM

Douglas Van Dorn

The Unseen Realm: Q & A Companion
Edited by Michael Heiser.
Published by Lexham Press.

In *The Unseen Realm*, Dr. Michael S. Heiser unpacked 15 years of research while exploring what the Bible really says about the supernatural world. That book has nearly 900 reviews and a five-star rating. It is a game-changer

Doug helps you further explore *The Unseen Realm* with a fresh perspective and an easy-to-follow format. The book summarizes key concepts and themes from Heiser's book and includes questions aimed at helping you gain a deeper understanding of the biblical author's supernatural worldview.

The format is that of a catechism: A Question followed by the Answer. There are 95 Questions (nod to Martin Luther) divided into 12 Parts:

Part I—God
Part II—The Lesser Gods
Part III—The Sons of God
Part IV—Divine Council
Part V—Sin, Rebellion, and the Fall
Part VI—Rebellion before the flood
Part VII—Rebellion after the flood
Part VIII—The Promise Anticipated
Part IX—The Promise Fulfilled
Part X—The Good News

Available in Paperback or Kindle at Amazon.com or on the Bible-software platform Logos at Logos.com

From the Shadows to the Savior:
Christ in the Old Testament

Few subjects are as important--yet ignored or misapplied--as the one addressed in this book. Jesus Christ is the absolute center and focus of the totality of God's word. Many people confess this belief, since Jesus himself taught it (Luke 24:27; John 5:39). Christians have done well to see this on one or two levels, yet truly understanding just how primary he is as an actor—even in the Old Testament—is something few have considered.

In this book, adapted from a series of blog posts for the Decablog, Doug helps us see the light of Christ that emerges from the dark hallways of Scriptures that so many find outdated, unintelligible, and irrelevant for today's Church.

Learn how Christ is found in such things as prophecy, typology, and the law. Then, come in for a deeper study of how the Person himself is actually present, walking, speaking, and acting, beginning in the very first book of the Bible. Learn how words such as "Word," "Name," "Glory," and "Wisdom" are all ideas that the Scripture itself attaches to Christ who in the OT is called The Angel of the LORD. Then see if such ideas don't radically change the way you think about all of God's word in this truly life-changing summary of Christ in the Old Testament.

Chapters:
NT Passages and Reflections
Christ in Prophecy
Christ in Typology
Christ and the Law
Christ: The Angel of the LORD
Christ: The Word of God
Christ: The Name of the LORD
Christ: The Wisdom of God
Christ: The Son of God
Christ: The Glory of God
Christ: The Right Arm of God

Available in Paperback or Kindle at Amazon.com

Waters of Creation:
A Biblical-Theological Study of Baptism

This is the one book on baptism that you must read. It was seven years in the making. Doug believes that until a new approach is taken, separations over the meaning, mode, and recipients of baptism will never be bridged.

This new approach traces the roots of baptism deep into the OT Scriptures. When understood properly, we discover that baptism is always the sign that God has used to initiate his people into a new creation. Baptism in the NT is not "new." Rather, it derives its origin from OT predecessors. It has a direct, sacramental counterpart, and it isn't circumcision. It is baptism. When we understand that baptism comes from baptism, especially in its sacramental expression in the priestly covenant, reasons for the NT practice begin to make perfect sense.

Now Baptists have an argument that infant Baptists can finally understand, because we are beginning our argument in the same place. This is an Old Testament covenantal approach to the Baptist position with baptistic conclusions as to the mode and recipients of baptism. That's what happens when we root baptism in baptism rather than circumcision.

Chapters:
The Baptism of Jesus
Baptism and the Sanctuary
Baptism and the Priesthood
Baptism and the Covenant
Implications for Christian Baptism

Available in Paperback or Kindle at Amazon.com

Covenant Theology:
A Reformed Baptist Primer

Covenant theology is often said to be the domain of infant Baptists alone. But there really are such things as Reformed Baptists who believe in covenant theology as a basic system for approaching Scripture.

This primer sets out to give the basics of a Reformed Baptist covenant theology and to do so in a way that is understandable to the uninitiated. It was originally a series we did on Sunday nights at our church. It agrees with classical formulations of covenant theology in that there is a Covenant of Redemption, a Covenant of Works, and a Covenant of Grace in the Bible.

The book takes a multi-perspective approach to the Covenant of Redemption in that this covenant is the basis for the classic formula that Christ's death is sufficient for all, but efficient for the elect. It sees the Covenant of Works for Adam in a broader context of a covenant made with all of creation, a covenant where laws establish the parameters for creation's existence.

It differs from Paedobaptist covenant theology in that it sees the Covenant of Grace as only properly coming through Jesus Christ. OT gracious covenants are typological of the Covenant of Grace but save people on the basis of the coming work of Christ through faith alone. This is the traditional way Reformed Baptists have articulated the Covenant of Grace.

Finally, it sees an entire covenant in the Old Testament as often (but not always) missing from formulations of covenant theology. In the opinion of the author, this "priestly covenant" is vital to a proper understanding of 1. The continuity of the practice of baptism from OT to NT, 2. The answer to why we never find infants being baptized in the NT, and 3. A more precise way to parse the legal aspects of the OT economy, thereby helping us understand why the moral law continues today. This volume works from the basic presupposition that continuity in God's word is more basic than discontinuity. In this, it differs from dispensationalism and new covenant theology. The book suggests that this is the greatest strength of covenant theology, which does also recognize discontinuity.

Available in Paperback or Kindle at Amazon.com

Galatians:
A Supernatural Justification

A play on words, the subtitle of this book gives you the two main points it tries to get across. Galatians central message teaches how a person is *justified* before a holy God. This once precious and central teaching of Protestant theology is often misunderstood or relegated the pile of irrelevant, stale doctrine.

Perhaps that is why the Apostle Paul supercharges his teaching with an oft-overlooked side of this letter - the *supernatural* beings who tempt us and teach us to give up the only truth that will save us. Galatian Christians would have been familiar with these supernatural beings; their culture was steeped in it. Thus, they mistake Paul for the messenger-healer god Hermes, and Barnabas for Zeus. Paul's warning: "Even if we or an angel from heaven should preach to you a gospel contrary to the one we preached to you, let him be accursed." This is Paul's fatherly way of showing his children in the faith that the gospel is paramount; it alone is able to save. Such a warning like this can have new power, as people are returning with reckless abandon to the worship of the old gods.

This book is from a series of sermons preached at the Reformed Baptist Church of Northern Colorado in 2011.

Available in Paperback or Kindle at Amazon.com

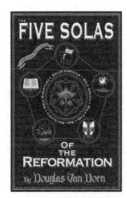

The Five Solas
of the Reformation

The 500th anniversary of the Reformation occurred in 2017. It was October 31, 1517 that Martin Luther nailed his 95 Thesis to the door of the great cathedral at Wittenberg, Germany. He had no idea what that simple act would do. His bold proclamation and challenge to for Rome to reform her ways and beliefs was met with hostility from some and great sympathy from others. Out of this sympathy arose Protestantism, a movement deeply concerned with grounding all things on Holy Scripture, giving glory to God alone, and recovering for that generation the biblical gospel of Jesus Christ. In five chapters, Doug Van Dorn takes us back to these ancient catchphrases that once moved a continent. Scripture Alone, Grace Alone, Faith Alone, Christ Alone, and To God Be the Glory Alone became the rallying cry of all who longed to see men and women, boys and girls saved and set free from sin, death, and the devil. The end of the book contains four helpful Appendices on songs, Church Fathers on the solas, a bibliography for further research, and a letter from Martin Luther.

Available in Paperback or Kindle at Amazon.com

Made in the USA
Las Vegas, NV
09 January 2025

16140151R00095